ROUTLEDGE LIBRARY EDITIONS: LOGIC

Volume 24

THE PROBLEMS OF LOGIC

THE PROBLEMS OF LOGIC

ANDREW PAUL USHENKO

LONDON AND NEW YORK

First published in 1941 by George Allen & Unwin Ltd

This edition first published in 2020
by Routledge
2 Park Square, Milton Park, Abingdon, Oxon OX14 4RN

and by Routledge
52 Vanderbilt Avenue, New York, NY 10017

Routledge is an imprint of the Taylor & Francis Group, an informa business

© 1941 Andrew Paul Ushenko

All rights reserved. No part of this book may be reprinted or reproduced or utilised in any form or by any electronic, mechanical, or other means, now known or hereafter invented, including photocopying and recording, or in any information storage or retrieval system, without permission in writing from the publishers.

Trademark notice: Product or corporate names may be trademarks or registered trademarks, and are used only for identification and explanation without intent to infringe.

British Library Cataloguing in Publication Data
A catalogue record for this book is available from the British Library

ISBN: 978-0-367-41707-9 (Set)
ISBN: 978-0-367-81582-0 (Set) (ebk)
ISBN: 978-0-367-42253-0 (Volume 24) (hbk)
ISBN: 978-0-367-42647-7 (Volume 24) (pbk)
ISBN: 978-0-367-85438-6 (Volume 24) (ebk)

Publisher's Note
The publisher has gone to great lengths to ensure the quality of this reprint but points out that some imperfections in the original copies may be apparent.

Disclaimer
The publisher has made every effort to trace copyright holders and would welcome correspondence from those they have been unable to trace.

THE PROBLEMS OF LOGIC

by

ANDREW PAUL USHENKO

London
GEORGE ALLEN AND UNWIN LTD

FIRST PUBLISHED IN 1941

ALL RIGHTS RESERVED
PRINTED IN GREAT BRITAIN
in 12-Point Old Face Type
BY UNWIN BROTHERS LIMITED
WOKING

CONTENTS

CHAPTER		PAGE
I.	THE NATURE OF LOGIC	9
II.	THE PARADOXES OF LOGIC	47
III.	CONSISTENCY AND THE DECISION-PROBLEM	87
IV.	CONCEPTUAL REFERENCE	117
V.	LOGIC AND REALITY	152
VI.	THE EXISTENCE OF PROPOSITIONS	198
	INDEX	223

Chapter 1

THE NATURE OF LOGIC

§ 1. Introduction

Ideas about the nature of logic, when they do not develop from a working experience of problems within logic, are likely to be "empty and jejeune", and it might appear sensible to begin by merely saying that logic is a theory concerned with such and such problems, viz. the problems that contemporary logicians are trying to solve, and then proceed with a discussion of these special problems. But as things happen to stand now this would be an extremely dangerous, if not a disastrous, course to take. For the particular logical problems of to-day are specialized to the extent of being highly technical points of symbolic calculus, and if they should become the only concern of logic, logic would become a science, more precisely a branch of mathematics. This is, of course, just what the majority of contemporary logicians, who are at their best mathematicians, believe logic must be. They like to remind us that philosophers were responsible, as was recognized by Kant himself in a famous passage (which, however, was not intended to be used for condemning logic), for the century-long stagnation of formal logic, and that to stir it up to its present state of feverish activity (carried on by a yearly increasing number of adepts), mathematicians,

The Problems of Logic

Boole, Peirce, De Morgan, Peano, Schröder, Russell, etc., had to take the matter in their hands. From this point of view logic, to be alive, must be symbolic or mathematical.

I have called the activity of symbolic logicians "feverish", but I do not know whether this should imply the delicate question whether it signifies the momentum or the inertia of logical research. We must not forget that the results of a similar activity of mediaeval logicians have been scored under the name of scholasticism throughout the subsequent ages. However, I am willing to admit that in the main symbolic logic is an improvement upon the Aristotelean tradition. And it is certain that in making a definition of logic we must take account of the development of technical exercises in symbolic calculus. Even more, we must do justice to the interests of to-day and put the technical aspect of logic in the foreground. But I still take exception to the "greed" of the mathematical logician when he identifies the technical aspect with the whole of logic or when he decides that because of the prominence of mathematicians in all recent developments of logic it is time to have the latter transferred from the competence of philosophy to the departments of mathematics. This brings a vital issue before both philosophy and logic, and because of it a discussion of the status of logic cannot be merely academic. Philosophy has suffered many amputations. The most recent of those, the segregation of psychology into an independent science, has proved to have been a procedure of very doubtful value.

The Nature of Logic

Hence my concern is not simply a personal grudge of a philosopher against the success of mathematicians; I feel that an act of violence against the natural union of philosophy and logic is about to be perpetrated. And I shall argue the natural character of their union. I believe that an exclusively mathematical treatment cannot give an adequate account of logic.

A fundamental characteristic of logic is *comprehensiveness*. This brings out the affinity between logic and philosophy, for to be comprehensive is the aim of philosophical ambition. Philosophers are so interested in categories, such as substance, relation, and the like, because these are comprehensive concepts the application of which not only transcends the confines of special sciences and arts, but is not even hampered by the barriers between human endeavours and processes of raw nature. Logical forms are, even more than philosophical categories, independent of the variations in their subject-matter or content: they have a claim to universal application. From this point of view it is very difficult to construe logic as a science, for mere sciences are always specialized. In fact scientific success is an outcome of specialization. This is particularly true of sciences which, like mathematics, take the form of *postulational systems*.* A postulational system is,

---

* It is likely that sciences must always take a postulational form as soon as they reach a high degree of exactitude. For example, the procedure of physical theory, according to Mr. R. B. Lindsay, "is to start from certain intuitive and logically indefinable concepts and from these to build more elaborate concepts by purely postulational

of course, worked out as an *abstract structure* and can be contrasted with its *interpretations* which are taken from various fields of actuality. Nevertheless the construction of different postulational systems is not only guided by the natural segregation of the fields of interpretation into distinct groups, but it must be made flexible enough to allow for the incessant differentiation and specialization of sub-groupings within the already established groups. The postulational method is adopted by the scientist because of the ease with which it responds to the increasing specialization; it responds by a mere addition of new postulates to the original set. For example, the postulates for serial order are, to begin with, tools for grouping together such various things as natural numbers in their succession of increasing magnitude, Kings of England in their chronological succession, and so on. But the practical importance of this set of postulates is the fact that with an addition of a new postulate it can single out a special type of series, for instance, the type of dense series which are interpretable, among other things, as fractions in their order of magnitude. The adjustment of

methods. . . . It is not denied, to be sure, that ideas gained from experience and in particular laboratory operations enter into this process. Inevitably, however, there is and always will be an element of arbitrary choice in the construction of concepts: we build those which we believe are going to be useful to us in physical description, even if they do not always correspond closely to raw experience. . . . Having constructed the concepts and assigned symbols to them, we continue the process of theory building by assuming certain mathematical relations among the symbols. . . ." Cf. "Operationalism in Physics", *Philosophy of Science*, October 1937, p. 459.

The Nature of Logic

postulational systems to the persevering desire for specialization is so striking that one can venture to conjecture that postulational treatment is essentially a method of differentiation. And this conjecture has a further confirmation whenever postulational development must perforce be carried out without the aid of interpretation. The splitting of geometry into euclidean and non-euclidean varieties is, of course the memorable instance. If so, it is only natural to expect that a thorough application of the postulational treatment to logic would run contrary to its essential claim to comprehensiveness. Indeed a differentiation of logic in the hand of mathematicians is exactly what has happened. First, there are different systems of mathematical logic.* Even if they were translatable into one another, they would not be comprehensive systems because their intertranslation cannot be performed within either of them, but presupposes a neutral medium, such as English, with a non-mathematical logic embedded in it. Secondly, there are *alternative mathematical logics* which cannot even be reduced to one another. The discovery of alternative logics may be a positive achievement, but it, certainly, means that classical logic, as an interpretation of the two-valued alternative system, has rivals and must relinquish its monopoly upon the valid forms of thought. Of course, the relationships among alternative logics are not yet made entirely clear. But, again, the very fact that problems about them are raised proves that

* For example, there is the Boolean algebra of logic, the system of the Principia, Curry's Combinatory logic, Church's system, etc.

The Problems of Logic

these alternative systems are not comprehensive. Their relationships must be established within a neutral medium with a non-mathematical logic embedded in it.

I do not for a moment doubt that forms of deduction can be exhibited in full by the postulational method. But formal logic is not the whole of logic. There is besides the *theory of logic*. This is the medium in which an introduction as well as a discussion of logical forms and of symbolic notation must take place. And it must, at least in part, consist of non-symbolic and non-formal statements.* For symbols have to be explained, the various modes of their combinations noted, and the rules for the derivation of certain complexes of symbols (theorems) from others (postulates) expressed. Furthermore, the given symbolic system of logic must be compared, as we have already seen, with other symbolic logics, whether reducible to one another or alternative. Of course, these facts cannot be altogether denied even by the advocates of the thoroughly mathematicized logic. The disagreement comes through a twist of interpretation which they can give to the facts. They recognize the difference between formal logic and the theory of logic, but, instead of taking it as a distinction between an exhibition and a description of the forms of actual discourse, they treat it as an actual separation of systems. Accordingly the theory of logic is said to be not a part of logic at all but a *separate system* which under the name of *metalogic* or *syntax-language* is then contrasted with the symbolic

* Cf. W. E. Johnson, *Logic*, v. 2, ch. iii, pp. 2 and 3.

The Nature of Logic

postulational system (which is the object of metalogical discussion) to be known as the *object-logic* or the *object-language* or, simply, as logic. This separation between metalogic and logic does not require, on the other hand, that the former should be given in terms of ordinary non-formal language. It is suggested that dependence on ordinary language and its intuitive logic in the matter of exposition of symbolism is a contingency of human civilization, since one can conceive of other beings, such as Martians, who would have a native ability to think along the lines of a symbolic calculus. Furthermore, after a sufficiently resourceful symbolic language had been introduced one can even formulate within it most of its own syntax, much as the syntax of English is formulated in English.* This does not mean, however, that the separation between syntax and its object can be dispensed with. The syntax-language is always more comprehensive than the object-language, for, as the work of Gödel, Carnap, Tarski, and others has shown, some of the metalogical statements must remain untranslatable into the expressions of the object-language. At the same time, although more comprehensive than formal logic, metalogic cannot play the part of a comprehensive system, because metalogic is itself an object for analysis and therefore presupposes a still more comprehensive meta-metalogic, which in its turn is

* It is sometimes said that the formulation of the syntax within the object-language is inconsistent with their separation. This is not so. The formulas of the object-language, regardless of what they "express", remain distinct from their syntactical interpretation.

the object of a meta-meta-metalogic, and so on *ad infinitum*. This awkward assumption of an unending hierarchy of logics is, to my mind, a distorted analogue of the claim to comprehensiveness in intuitive logic, *necessarily* distorted by the mathematical treatment.

But let us defer criticism to a context in which a closer examination of metalogic is possible. In this Introduction the need is for a mere illustration of the striking divergence of the two contemporary views on the status of logic. These opposing views will be referred to as the *intuitional* and the *postulational* theories, and their respective adherents as the *intuitionalists* and the *postulationalists*.* To further the cause of the intuitional theory is the main purpose of this essay.

§ 2. Logic and Metalogic

The intuitional theory is not hostile to the use of symbols in logic. But while the postulationalists segregate the symbols in use into an *isolated calculus* or language, the object-logic, the intuitionalists take these same symbols as a *part of English* (or of whatever other common language the logician happens to speak), a sort of shorthand intended to avoid recourse to technical terms or a construction of

---

* The intuitional theory of logic must not be confused with the *intuitionism* of the *intuitionist* Brouwer, in which the two-valued logic is co-extensive with the field of finite aggregates. The postulational theory is a designation which applies both to the *formalism* of Hilbert's school and to the linguistic theory of logic of *logical positivism*.

The Nature of Logic

cumbersome statements. Take, for example, the formula:

(1) $p \lor \sim p$.

To the intuitionalist this is a symbolic expression of the traditional principle of the excluded middle and an abbreviation of what can be put in words as:

(1') A proposition is either true or false.

Such symbols as "wedge" and "curl" are obviously used in (1) as ideographical for the logical constants "either-or" and "it is false that", which are phrases in plain English. As to the variables p, q, etc., they do not function as abbreviations directly, but by *representing* any of the indefinite number of English propositions they secure brevity of expression even to a greater extent than the symbols for logical constants. The fact that in effect the variables are merely devices of abbreviation must be plain since, as the comparison of (1) and (1') illustrates, the same logical principles which are given as symbolic formulas can be expressed at a greater length by means of such technical terms as "proposition" without making any use of variables.

In the postulational treatment formula (1) is merely a complex of marks written down in a combination which is allowed for by the rules of the symbolic calculus within its context. A "postulate" or a "theorem" are just technical names for such a combination where it can be used within the system without restriction. A "variable" like "p" is then an element-mark in a symbolic formation

The Problems of Logic

for which other marks can be substituted under specified conditions. The connection which a postulational system of logic can have with propositions in actual discourse is established outside the system by *interpretation*. A mark like "p" by itself does not represent anything, therefore it does not represent a proposition, but we can, if we choose, *interpret* it as a proposition. We might, however, interpret it as "house" or as any other word provided one condition is satisfied: an interpretation of a "postulate" or a "theorem" in terms of English words must describe a situation which, conventionally or otherwise, is assertible as a fact.

The postulationalist divorce of a symbolic language from its interpretation in English or from any other syntax-language is supposed to give a twofold gain in the generality of treatment. First, it leaves the possibility of important interpretations of symbolic formulas other than in terms of propositions. Second, it provides for a construction of alternative systems which after they are interpreted in English would give non-aristotelean modes of argument. In mathematics a similar claim to a twofold advantage of the postulational approach has been, no doubt, well founded.* But in symbolic logic the possibility of new interpretations remains so far merely theoretical. As to non-aristotelean logics, although they might have been introduced as postulational sys-

---

* Non-euclidean geometry is the classical example of a mathematical discipline which was discovered through generality and independence of intuition in the application of the postulational method.

The Nature of Logic

tems, actually they were discovered by means of the extension of the truth-table method.* But the real difficulty with the attempts to keep logic separate from metalogic is that they cannot succeed because in a disguised form logic must reappear as a part of metalogic. One must remember that metalogic is *concerned* with logic, it is defined as the theory of the symbolic calculus, viz. as a discussion of the correctness of formulas and of their deducibility as theorems, of symbolic *formation* and *transformation*. In such a metalogical discussion reference to the formulas concerned must take place almost at every step. But since these formulas belong to the object-logic they cannot be referred to, i.e. reproduced within the metalogical discussion without becoming thereby an actual part of metalogic. In order to avoid the full force of this objection the postulationalists hold that without being directly referred to, the original formulas can be discussed by means of *metalogical replicas* of their structure. However, in actual practice these metalogical replicas are simply reproductions of the object-formulas, only given in quotation marks. Let the formula of the object-logic be:

(2) $\qquad p \supset p.$

In metalogic (2) is discussed by means of "$p \supset p$"

---

* It is true that the postulationalists can interpret the construction of various truth-tables as a metalogical or syntactical procedure in the exhibition of various combinations of such meaningless marks as T and F. But this was not the original interpretation. To Wittgenstein, for example, T and F are meaningful abbreviations for the propositional truth-values, "truth" and "falsehood".

or '$p \supset p$'. The use of double or single inverted commas indicates that the postulationalist deals with the metalogical representation of and not with the original expression (2). Thus while the intuitionalist would say "one of the theorems of logic is $p \supset p$", the postulationalists must say "One of the theorems of the object-logic is '$p \supset p$'". And the net result of this practice is that almost all of the object-logic is duplicated under the "protection" of quotation marks as a part of metalogic. In fact this duplication has usurped the functions of the original logic to the extent of making the latter practically unusable. Thus in recent works in logic the actual deduction of theorems from postulates within the object-logic gives way to a metalogical or syntactical method of deciding with regard to formulas in quotation marks whether or not they are deducible. And even when it comes to carrying out a proof, one might find the ". . . more fruitful method to be that of proving universal syntactical sentences. . . . Sometimes the proof . . . can be effected by the construction of a *schema* for the proof".[*] I suppose the postulationalist might agree with me that there is a virtual duplication of logic within metalogic, yet he would insist that the two must be kept apart at least in principle, for, as long as they are kept separate, he has the satisfaction of treating symbols as mere marks on the paper, which saves him from entanglement in interpretation while operating with the symbols. But I think that even this satisfaction, doubtful as it

[*] R. Carnap, *The Logical Syntax of Language*, Kegan Paul, 1937, p. 53.

The Nature of Logic

is, must be denied to the postulationalist the very moment that he makes use of his schemas for proof instead of carrying out actual proofs within the object-logic. For as a means of avoiding the intuitionalist interpretation of the symbols, p, q, etc., as variables, i.e. as representatives of propositions in discourse, some such device as the enclosure of these symbols in quotation marks is in order. For example, the metalogical expression "$p \supset p$" does not contain variables because it is in quotation marks, which means that the letter involved in it is not a representative but a name of the letter in formula (2). But the metalogical *schemas* are not symbolic expressions in quotation marks. As defined by Bernays, a formula-schema is "a rule saying that every formula of a certain kind of composition can be taken as a starting formula" in the object-language.*
It follows that a schema is concerned with *kinds* of things rather than with *individual* things such as strings of marks on the paper, and therefore when symbols are employed in the formulation of a schema they must represent rather than name individual marks. Thus if the metalogical formula schema $(A.B) \supset A$ tells us that every formula with the same structure can be a starting formula in the object-logic, this is another way of saying that the schema represents the starting formulas of the object logic exemplified by: $(p \cdot q) \supset p$; $(q \cdot r) \supset q$, etc. The capital letters of the schema are variables relatively to the small letters of the formulas within the

* Cf. *Logical Calculus*, 1935–36, The Institute for Advanced Study, Princeton, p. 41.

The Problems of Logic

object-logic. For instance, A represents p or q or any other symbol following the horseshoe of the exemplifications. Now the schemas are not only admitted, but have an extensive use, in metalogic. And since this amounts to a large-scale operation with variables, there should be no objection against treating all sentential symbols as variables. Such a treatment would do away with the mass of quotation marks as well as with the whole object-logic mediating between the theory of form and the forms of actual discourse. This, of course, would mean a rejection of the postulationalist standpoint in favour of the intuitionalist theory. But the postulationalist is not likely to be intimidated by notational inconvenience, he is even ready to face another and much more formidable complication. Metalogic is supposed to be concerned with object-logic while dealing with its own expressions in quotation marks and not with the corresponding expressions of logic without quotation marks. Of course, we are told that the two sets of expressions are in correspondence, that the metalogical set represents the logical set, but the difficulty remains that a statement of such a correspondence cannot be made either in metalogic or in logic. For example, the statement that "$p \supset q$" *is a metalogical designation of the formula* $p \supset q$ cannot be made in metalogic which has no way of writing the formula and it cannot be made in logic which does not use quotation marks. The hierarchy of metalogics would not be of any help either because although each of them is concerned with a less comprehensive language, none can quote expressions of its object-language directly, i.e. without quotation marks. The postulationalists themselves saw the point, and one of them, Alfred Tarski, has offered a solution in the construction of his "semantics" which is an additional language designed to mediate between logic and metalogic. Naturally this raises a host of new questions, and, for the present at least, Tarski's solution looks more like an over-complication of an already involved case.

One reason why the postulationalists persist in their practice is their conviction that the intuitionalist use of symbolic expressions without quotation marks is bound to result in confusion. Carnap speaks of the necessity for a notational discrimination between the symbol and the symbolized object "when the designated object is itself a linguistic expression".* Nevertheless it is significant that some mathematical logicians, for example Hilbert and Ackerman in their text-book *Grundzüge der teoretischen Logik*, neglect notational distinctions between the symbol and the symbolized without being in the least confusing.† From the intuitionalist standpoint there should even be no danger of confusion. So far as the symbols of logical constants are concerned, the dot, the wedge, etc., they need not

* Op. cit., p. 153.

† A reviewer of the second edition of the work of Hilbert and Ackerman writes in *The Journal of Philosophy*, July 7, 1938: "The authors themselves call attention to the difference between discoursing *with* a symbol and discoursing *about* one. It is a distinction which is fundamental to the work of the Hilbert school, and can be violated in general only at the price of confusion." The reviewer, however, has nowhere shown that there is a confusion in the book reviewed.

The Problems of Logic

be distinguished from the corresponding connectives of discourse, "and", "either-or", etc., because both sets are logically equivalent, their contributions to conceptual articulation within their respective contexts are the same. As to the variables p, q, etc., they cannot be confused with a particular sentence of discourse, because they do not name particular sentences but represent any of them indiscriminately. The intuitionalist, therefore, can reserve expressions in quotation marks for his own purpose of distinguishing between two uses of symbols which are exactly analogous to William of Occam's *significative* and *insignificative* employment of words. The distinction can be illustrated by a pair of statements of which one gives a significative and the other an insignificative function to the same symbol: p represents any proposition; "p" looks like "q" which is turned around. Strictly speaking, formal logic is concerned with the significative use of symbols only, but in the theory of logic one might sometimes need a description of their perceptual appearance. It is hardly necessary to explain that the admission of significative symbols and terms does not mean that intuitional logic is intensional. For in further agreement with the terminology and spirit of William of Occam, the intuitionalist can hold that the terms of logic, although significant, do not designate actual things but are terms of *second intention*, i.e. they are about such modes of signification as proposition, predicate, and the like.* Let me illustrate the point.

* As an exception I can mention the "objective for reference" to be discussed along with the problem of conceptual reference.

The Nature of Logic

When one asserts that "the earth is round" one uses a proposition, but not as a logician does, one is concerned not with propositions but with the earth and its roundness, which are extra-logical actualities; the particular proposition is exclusively in terms of first intention. But when it is said that "every proposition is either true or false", this principle although having a bearing upon the assertion that "the earth is round" as well as upon any other particular statement, is not directly concerned with the earth or with any other manifestation of actuality: it is about propositions taken formally and not about their subject-matter, and therefore it is a principle of logic. Occam's doctrine of terms of second intention is a key to understanding the intuitionalist treatment of that part of logic which I have called the theory of form in distinction from the exhibition of transformation of logical structures into one another.

§ 3. LOGIC AS THE THEORY OF FORM

The intuitionalist understanding of logic as a symbolic exhibition and a theory of form has the weight of history behind it. Aristotelean logic was its first version and the system of the *Principia Mathematica* its culmination. It is true that the logistic method of the *Principia* is *semi-postulational*: nothing but explicitly stated primitive propositions and rules of deduction are allowed in the derivation of its theorems. But the primitive propositions are not postulates constructed by convention, they are principles about form which are recognized to be true by logical intuition, i.e. by direct inspection and without regard to empirical matters.

Logical intuition is of two kinds, either immediate perception of significance; i.e. a discrimination between significant and insignificant conceptual structures, or immediate recognition of what Whitehead calls a validating form, i.e. of a form which in its particular exemplifications can give only true propositions regardless of their subject-matter.

Significance is taken here in opposition to connotation. The significance of a term or of a construct is its contribution to the articulation and unity of a conceptual context in abstraction from connotative meaning. Contribution to conceptual unity varies in degree. It may enable a logical entity to stand out as a complete form even in isolation from a more comprehensive context. The significance of a proposition illustrates such an independence of context. A proposition can, of course, function in co-operation with other propositions in discourse, but it also must be completely intelligible when it stands by itself. This is why propositions are called units of thought, whereas their constituents (which are not propositions) have only a contextual significance. But the majority of logical entities enjoy distinctness not as a capacity to stand by themselves but as a transferability from one context to another. For example, the logical connective "if-then" is significant only within an implication, but it has the same significance as we go from one implication to

The Nature of Logic

another. When significance does not reach the maximum of being self-complete or unified, it is a contribution to the articulation of some complete context. The independence of connotative meaning which such a contribution to articulation has can best be explained by means of illustrations. "All cars have wheels" and "All men have heads" differ in meaning but have the same significance, of a general proposition. Again "The touch of earthly years" and "The touch of girthly means" have the same significance, of a descriptive phrase, although the second expression is meaningless. Thus meaninglessness does not imply insignificance, but insignificance implies meaninglessness. It would be wrong to hold that "The sum of justice and painting is red", meaningless as it is, has the same significance as "The sum of two and three is computable". Observe that not only all the words of the meaningless expression have meaning but that the expression itself is grammatically and syntactically correct; if it is meaningless, this is because it is logically insignificant. Illustrations of this kind put us on guard against confusion between linguistic and logical significance. *"The syntax of language" is not the same thing as logical significance.* Terms which have an identical linguistic form can yet differ in their contribution to conceptual construction. Thus "red" and "computable" are both adjectives, but only the second can be attached with logical significance to the noun "sum". Logic is concerned with discrimination among *conceptual kinds* even when language gives no clue to their distinction. Of course, linguistic distinctions of syntax have been devised in order to express logical distinctions of significance, but the correspondence is so inadequate that one can make use of their discrepancy both in defining form and in explaining logical analysis. Logical form can be defined as the order of distribution of conceptual significance among the elements of a context regardless of whether these elements are identical with or different from the elements of the verbal form through which the context is expressed. Logical analysis is directed by the discrepancy between the verbal and the logical forms in a search for a closer linguistic expression. Accordingly, logical analysis usually consists in the replacement of the original sentence to-be-analysed by another which does better justice to the conceptual distinctions of significance involved; it is a process of successive approximations to the exhibition of propositional form.* If, however, the postulationalists were right in their rejection of propositions, if sentences formed the sole object of logic, analysis

---

* A notable example of logical analysis is Russell's theory of definite description. Suppose the original sentence is "The criminal B is caught". This is analysed into a much more complicated sentence "There exists one criminal being designated as B and there are no others of the same designation and B is caught". If one asks why this complicated conjunction is any better than the original sentence, the answer is because it makes explicit the three conditions which satisfy the claim to truth of the original sentence. Now the claim to truth (as it will be proved later) is an element of the formal significance of a proposition, and therefore by stating explicitly the conditions of its satisfaction the latent elements of propositional form are brought out for inspection.

The Nature of Logic

would be forced to move along purely conventional lines, it would cease to have the importance of progress in self-clarification of thought and would degenerate into a mere game of verbal transformations.

The thesis that logical form is not co-extensive with the syntax of language, however comprehensive the latter may be, is the main point of difference between intuitionalism and the remarkable version of the postulational theory developed by Carnap. It is gratifying to note that Carnap approaches the intuitionalist position closer than any other postulationalist ever did. Carnap rejects the naïve view that the sentence is either merely a physical string of marks on the paper or even a class of such strings collected together because of the similarity of their design. For him ". . . the design (visual form, *Gestalt*) of the individual symbols is a matter of indifference".* Syntactically only *kinds* of symbols are important. Hence much as a sentence needs an embodiment in spoken or written words it is a rather conceptual set-up the constituents of which represent different syntactical kinds. "For instance, given an appropriate rule, it can be proved that the word-series 'Pirots karulize elatically' is a sentence, provided only that 'Pirots' is known to be a substantive (in the plural), 'karulize' a verb (in the third person plural), and 'elatically' an adverb. . . ."† If, furthermore, one makes allowance for Carnap's extension of the meaning of "syntax", it becomes obvious that

* Op. cit., p. 6.
† Op. cit., p. 2.

The Problems of Logic

his syntactical kinds are practically indistinguishable from the intuitionalist explicit forms of logic, and his sentences play the part of propositional structures (i.e. of propositions taken in abstraction from their connotative content). Yet, even if we leave aside the implicit forms, there remains a difference in principle: on Carnap's premise that syntactical kinds and rules are constructions of arbitrary convention the adequacy of a linguistic translation of the intuitionalist logic must be an historical accident. And so long as we feel that logic cannot be at the mercy of historical accidents, we express our preference for intuitionalism over the linguistic theory. This is a natural feeling, and its force is even stronger when it comes to the recognition of validating forms than in the perception of significance. Carnap is entirely consistent when he treats the deduction of a conclusion from its premise as a mere linguistic transformation of one sentence into another. But, if the rules of transformation are entirely arbitrary, his account does not explain the fact of our awareness that denial of a valid deduction is inconceivable. Even Russell, in spite of his recent leanings to conventionalism, testifies to his intuition of validating forms: "It seems to me that these axioms either do, or do not, have the characteristic of formal truths which characterizes logic. . . . I confess, however, that I am unable to give any clear account of what is meant by saying that a proposition is 'true in virtue of its form'."* Apart from clarification derived

* B. Russell, *The Principles of Mathematics*, George Allen & Unwin Ltd., 1938, p. xii.

The Nature of Logic

from the doctrine of significance, there is no need for a clear account when logical intuition is operative. The ultimate basis of validating forms is intuition. There exists a capacity of discernment between a valid argument and a logical error.

We do not need to enquire whether intuition is in some sense innate or, if not, how it can be acquired; these are questions of psychology. But as advocates of intuitional logic we must answer a critic who points out that "principles" are known to have enjoyed for some time in the history of logic the prestige of intuitive certainty only to be denounced later as delusions. It is the infallibility of intuition which is in question. But the intuitionalist need not be troubled with the problem in such a sweeping form, it is enough if he can answer "yes" to the more restricted question whether intuition is trustworthy to the extent of serving as a basis for logic. The intuitionalist claims that under *specifiable* conditions his intuition is infallible, although he realizes that their actual specification is by no means easy. Perhaps Descartes' clarity and distinctness form the first approximation towards such a specification, although a present-day writer might prefer a formulation according to which intuition is reliable when the conceptual complex with which it is concerned is fully analysed. But at least one psychological requirement must be added: all elements relevant to the understanding of the complex must be capable of being grasped together within the span of concentrated attention. Whether one actually has in mind everything relevant is again for the intuition to decide. And psychologically this complication is so serious that one cannot expect anything but very primitive logical structures to be subject to an infallible pronouncement of intuition. Thus we can assert, confident of no error, the principle expressed by "$p \supset p$", since its import is made conceptually clear. But intuition becomes less reliable with the increasing complication within the conceptual object, and to counteract our wavering feeling of certainty we are sometimes forced to put our confidence into various artificial devices, among which a purely mechanical symbolic computation is of great value. The fact is that intuitive decision is relative to information on hand and as such it is not unlike the judgment of probability. It is well known that there may be several different and yet correct estimations of the probability of the same event, provided these estimations are based on different amounts of evidence. In the same way intuition may be at variance with its previous decision and yet remain correct because its changeability is conditioned by an accumulation in the data of analysis. If analysis is insufficient or lacks precision, logic may suffer, and sometimes it has suffered. But the danger of a faulty logic must not be exaggerated. For the "self-corrective" function of intuition springs into action automatically as soon as better analysis is available. Also while information is insufficient intuition has the "self-restraining" sense of passing judgment only upon elementary problems. This is why Aristotelean logic is so strikingly elementary and at the same time so remarkably free from bad

The Nature of Logic

mistakes. Furthermore intuition has often been held responsible for the faults of description. And although description may be derivative from some act of intuition, the two must be distinguished; in the process of derivation memory had taken the place of the original experience and when memory comes in there is no guarantee against error. Logical intuition is a direct apprehension of an exhibition of form, while logical description is an indirect account of form by means of words.

The distinction between an exhibition and a description of form is not incompatible with the existence of propositions which describe their own propositional form. There is, of course, no difficulty in having a proposition of a certain form which describes a different form of another proposition. A doubt arises only when a proposition describes its own form. And yet "self-description" would have to be the case, when a proposition which describes the form of another proposition happens to show the same form as the latter. Should Tweedledum describe the looks of Tweedledee, he would give a description of himself. Wittgenstein, who thought that a proposition cannot describe what it shows, was relying upon the "vicious-circle" principle of the theory of types that no proposition can be about itself. The separation of metalogic as descriptive of form from logic as form-exhibition was no doubt a development of Wittgenstein's position. Yet now that the postulationalists themselves have rejected the "vicious-circle" principle, they should realize that at least one corner-stone of their theory has crumbled.

The Problems of Logic

§ 4. The Principles of Extensionality and the Logic of Modality

Logic is an extensional system because deduction depends on formal properties and not, as the advocates of "intensional logic" hold, on connotation, i.e. on the sense or content of terms and propositions. The extensional nature of logic can best be expressed by the so-called postulates of extensionality. But this mode of expression must not be taken as a shift towards postulationalism. In the intuitionalist logic the "postulates" of extensionality are accepted as principles of logical intuition even though effective criticism of the attempts to base logical necessity upon connotation is required in order to clear the grounds for the intuition of extensionality.

There are two principles of extensionality; the first is operative within the calculus of unanalysed propositions, the other, which is the one usually called "the postulate of extensionality", is concerned with the calculus of predicates or propositional functions.

In the calculus of unanalysed propositions the ultimate terms are single propositions taken as units, i.e. without consideration of their more elementary constituents such as the subject or the predicate. Accordingly a symbol for a proposition is some single letter, usually "p" or "q" or "r" or "s" or "t". Since propositions thus symbolized are completely abstracted from connotation, they can be used for computation only in so far as their truth-value, i.e. their truth or falsehood, determines the truth-value,

The Nature of Logic

i.e. the truth or falsehood of the various combinations, the compound propositions, into which they enter as constituents. The first principle of extensionality guarantees the possibility of such computations:

Every compound proposition is a truth-function, i.e. its truth value is uniquely determined when definite truth-values are assigned to each of its constituents.

The calculus which ensues is therefore concerned with truth-values, in particular with the procedure of establishing which combinations of multiple truth or falsehood lead to truth and which to falsehood.

In a calculus of predicates abstraction from connotation has a notational expression in the use of predicate-variables or propositional functions instead of connotative adjectives (or relations). Now the latter are sometimes equivalent without being equal or interchangeable. Adjectives are equivalent if the predication of either of them with regard to the same subject (or individual) gives the same truth-values to the resulting propositions. For example, the characteristics "being an ex-King of England" and "being a Duke of Windsor" are equivalent, they are equally true of the same individual, and equally false of all others. Yet the two characteristics are not interchangeable: some people might know about the existence of the ex-King of England without knowing that at the present time he is the Duke of Windsor. But the only difference between these characteristics is connotative. Simi-

The Problems of Logic

larly for all other predicates, if they are equivalent they can differ only in connotation. Hence as long as logic in its use of symbols allows for the difference of equivalent characteristics it takes connotation into account and therefore is not purely extensional. To "purge" it from intensionality one must introduce the second principle, the so-called "postulate of extensionality":

If two or more predicates or propositional functions are equivalent, they are (for all purposes of logic) equal or interchangeable.

In conjunction the two principles of extensionality cover the whole field of formal logic, they assert in effect that identification of any logical expression, whether propositional or predicational, is determined by its truth-value.*

But are not these principles arbitrary? Do not they artificially restrict thought, and, if so, how can they be accepted by intuition?

The answer is that although an application of the principles of extensionality would put artificial restrictions upon the natural psychological course of thinking, they do not restrict logical deduction for

* In the calculus of classes a class is identified by its extension. For example, the class "man" is the same as the class "rational being"; the class "unicorn" is identical with the class "mermaid". Hence the calculus of classes needs no postulate of extensionality. But logicians have questioned the existence of classes and prefer to use instead propositional functions as logically unquestionable entities. Instead of using such a class as "man" they use such a propositional function as "human". The postulate of extensionality, without assuming the existence of classes, makes propositional functions "behave" as if they were classes.

The Nature of Logic

the simple reason that there can be no intensional deduction outside them. Logicians who profess to believe in intensional logical relations are usually confused: what they really have in mind is not intensional but modal logic, a logic in which, along with "true" and "false", there are modal adjectives, "possible", "necessary", "impossible", "contingent", and the like. A confusion between the logic of modality and intensional logic is inevitable when statements of modality are taken not in their proper and literal sense but as indirect expression of relationships growing out of the connotation of terms. This happens, for instance, when the statement "It is possible that the dog bites" is supposed to be merely a roundabout formulation of the statement "The dog might bite". But with a proper and literal interpretation the two statements should be kept apart. "The dog might bite" is intensional because it gives an intrinsic connotative correlation between "the dog" and "biting", a modification of terms within a single proposition. But as soon as the element of modality is pulled out of the original proposition and is prefixed in the form of the modal adjective "possible" to the proposition "the dog bites", it becomes a truth-qualification of this proposition taken as a whole, i.e. an extrinsic property of the proposition which is not concerned with its connotative constituents. In symbols the difference in question is expressed by giving to one of the statements the form "S might be P" which is not a completely formalized expression, and to the other the form "$\Diamond\, p$" (read "p is possible"), in which p is the symbol of an unanalysed proposition.

One might still think that although the modal adjectives can be separated from the connotative terms of the proposition to prefix the latter as a unit, they carry distinctions of connotation within themselves, since they are treated as modifiers, rather than as functions (which are themselves either true or false), of truth-value. If, for example, one needs a special sign, the diamond "$\Diamond$", to stand for "possible", the reason for this would seem to be the understanding that "possible" has a meaning of its own which is not reducible to truth-values or to other modal adjectives. This point has some importance as a reminder that modal logic is something more than the ordinary logic of truth and falsehood. But as a contention that modality is irreducible to truth-value and, in general, cannot be treated extensionally, it has been refuted in recent literature in three alternative approaches to the subject.

First, Carnap has shown that all specific modal properties can be translated into various syntactical characteristics of the forms within the object-language.* His method of translation can be illustrated by writing down a "dictionary" where the left-column gives the "intensional sentences of the logic of modalities" and the right-column their equivalent "extensional sentences of syntax":

A is possible   'A' is not contradictory
$A . \sim A$ is impossible   '$A . \sim A$' is contradictory

* Op. cit., §§ 67–8–9.

The Nature of Logic

$A \lor \sim A$ is necessary	'$A \lor \sim A$' is analytic
A strictly implies B	B is a logical consequence of A
etc.	etc.
etc.	etc.
etc.	etc.
etc.	etc.

The translations in the right-column are called "extensional sentences of syntax", because their characterizations are exclusively concerned with the form of the sentence which is abbreviated as 'A'. Of course, this method is conditioned by Carnap's distinction between the syntax and the object-language. But an intuitionalist can adjust the method to his own theory by introducing instead of the distinction between the syntax and the object-language a less drastic distinction between *characterization in words* and *exhibition in symbols* of the structure of a proposition or an argument. Thus, for example, while Carnap translates "$A \cdot \sim A$ is impossible" into "'$A \cdot \sim A$' is contradictory", in the intuitionalist readjustment the translation belongs not to syntax but to logic (or, if one prefers, it to the theory of logic) where "contradictory" is a descriptive characterization of the same form which '$A \cdot \sim A$' symbolically shows. If the logician feels some misgivings about such readjustment, for example, if he thinks that to characterize something as contradictory means to see intuitively that as a logical form it is impossible or inconceivable and that such an intuition discloses connotative qualifications, he still can

The Problems of Logic

be assured that the logic of modality is reducible to extensional logic if he turns to either of the other two procedures.*

One of them, the method of Lukasiewicz, is a representation of the logic of modality as a logic of truth-values. In order to do justice to modal characterizations and relationships which go beyond the ordinary logic of truth and falsehood, he has constructed *alternative logics* of more than two truth-values. The simplest of them is the three-valued logic. Whereas in the ordinary logic any given proposition p must have one of two values which can be symbolized by 1 and 0 and interpreted as "truth" and "falsehood", in the three-valued logic the same proposition p can take one of three values, either 1 or $1/2$ or 0. Let us interpret these three values as respectively, "necessary", "possible", and "impossible"; then the three-valued logic becomes a representation of a calculus of modality. To illustrate, let us take a statement about the future, "There will be a world-war in 1950." In the logic of truth and falsehood this statement is taken as either true or false with a qualification that at the present moment (in 1938) we do not know which it is. In the three-valued logic the same proposition could be either "true" or "false" only in the sense of being either "necessary" or "impossible", and since it obviously is neither, it is taken as merely "possible". Different

* An excellent exposition of the theory of the logics of modality will be found in the article "Les logiques nouvelles des modalités", by R. Feys. Cf. *Revue Néoscolastique de Philosophie*, October 1937, and May 1938.

The Nature of Logic

modal interpretations of the truth-values of the three-valued logic are, of course, possible. Lukasiewicz's own interpretation assigns to 1, $1/2$, 0 the adjectives "true", "possible", and "impossible", respectively. The restriction on these and all other interpretations is that the extreme values 1 and 0 cannot represent "truth" and "falsehood" at once. The reason is that "truth" and "falsehood", if used together, stand to one another in the relation of contradiction, but in the three-valued logic the contradictory of "p has the value 1" is not "p has the value 0" but "p has for its value either $1/2$ or 0", and the contradictory of "p has the value 0" is not "p has the value 1" but "p has for its value either $1/2$ or 1". The restriction on the interpretation of the truth-values does not mean that the representation of modality by an alternative logic must be incomplete. The modal-property which cannot be used as an interpretation of the original truth-values can always be introduced later as a function of an assignment of truth-values.* Nevertheless the restriction in question indicates that a many-valued logic cannot be identified with the logic of modality which it represents.† For the various truth-values of an alternative logic are *co-exclusive*, whereas modal properties sometimes even *entail* one another. For example, in modal logic a necessary proposition is also true, but in the three-valued logic a proposition whose value is 1 cannot have in addition the value

---

* "Les logiques nouvelles des modalités", by R. Feys. Cf. *Revue Néoscolastique de Philosophie*, October 1937, and May 1938, 88.42. † Ibid., 88.43.

The Problems of Logic

1/2. Hence if we interpret *1* as "necessary" this adjective would not have exactly the same meaning which the property necessary has when taken as a modification of truth. However, complete identification between the logic of modality and an extensional logic can be established by E. V. Huntington's method.*

Huntington's system deals with a class K of elements interpretable as ordinary propositions which are either true or false. But within K there is a subclass T which Huntington interprets as the class of assertible or deducible propositions and the postulation of which has the effect of segregating the necessary from the rest. Formally the symbols of modality are then defined in terms of the zero-element Z (the conjunction of two contradictory forms) and the binary operation "quad" which, when operative within the sub-class T, has all the properties of "equality". For example, "the impossibility of p" corresponds to "p quad Z", and "p is impossible", the assertion of impossibility, to "(p quad Z) is in T". In this manner C. I. Lewis's calculus of strict implication, which was originally offered as a logic of irreducible modality, is shown to have the same properties as Huntington's extensional system in which every expression is a truth-function while those of them that correspond to statements of

* "Postulates for Assertion, Conjunction, Negation, and Equality", *Proceedings of the American Academy of Arts and Sciences*, April 1937. A generalized form of Huntington's method was given by Dr. Fitch in his "Modal Functions in Two-Valued Logic", *Journal of Symbolic Logic*, September 1937.

The Nature of Logic

modality are defined in relation to the special subclass T.*

Granted that modal logic is extensional, whatever else passes under the name of intensional thinking is not strictly logical in the sense of objective and communicable demonstration. There are various ways of natural or psychological thinking which may have a compulsory force but only relatively to the particular minds who happen to entertain similar complexes of ideas, so that the compulsion felt cannot be identified with universal validity of logical conclusions. Even scientific inquiry, however indubitable are its results to the investigator, must be qualified as merely problematic because of the complex of assumptions peculiar to each science. Outside of non-formal reasoning touched with con-

---

* I think Mr. Fitch has generalized Huntington's procedure by defining modal properties relatively to any subset S (of the set K of all propositions of the two-valued logic), as its truth-functions, although he continues to use Huntington's special sub-class T. "The only restriction on S is that no member of S can occur in any other member of S. The representation (of modal properties) concerns the set $S K$ consisting of all members of K in which occur members of S. Every member of $S K$ may be regarded as a truth-function of the members of S. If S consists of only one member P, and if $f(P)$ and $g(P)$ are any members of $S K$, then we define $|f(P)|$ as $(f(P) . f(\sim P))$. The proposition '$f(P)$ is S-necessary' may then be expressed by $|f(P)|$."

"Thus is obtained a novel analysis of modality, contrasting, on the one hand, with Carnap's syntactic theory of modality, and, on the other hand, with Lewis's view of modal concepts as underivable from other logical concepts. We would maintain that modal concepts are not absolute, but always relative to some S, generally unspecified."

tingency, there exist thoughts which are related by connotation with undeniable necessity, but as far as I can judge from adduced examples, their relation does not allow for a genuine transition from a premise to a conclusion, but, if necessary, is merely a linguistic definition, i.e. an explication of the connotation of some word or phrase. Let us take from the advocates of "intensional logic" their favourite examples:

(1) A is red. Therefore it is coloured; (2) A is red. Therefore it is extended; (3) A is equilateral. Therefore it is equiangular; (4) A is a man. Therefore A cannot be his own son; (5) A is to the right of B. Therefore B is to the left of A.

The would-be deduction (1) is plainly a roundabout way of saying that the word "red" means, among other things, "coloured", a purely verbal statement of connotation. On the other hand, "red" does not connote the adjective "extended", and, therefore, (2) cannot be formulated as a verbal definition. Yet, for the same reason, (2) cannot be expressed in an analytic judgment, and, unless one is ready to take "Whatever is red is extended" as an instance of a Kantian synthetic judgment *a priori*, one must realize that it is not based on a necessary relation. Of course, in asserting that A is red, one can imagine a red patch as an illustration of this assertion, in which case the statement that A is extended is a description of the illustrative image, which would have the necessity of a psychological fact (viz. of the fact that one cannot visualize redness which is not spread through some area) but

The Nature of Logic

not of a logical conclusion. As soon as "red" is taken in abstraction from its psychological illustration and is used as an adjective that even a person born blind can understand, it even becomes debatable whether redness is always conceptually associated with extension. And if it were, the ground of association would not be logical necessity, but, as will be explained later, a semi-arbitrary system of categories, of which space is one, taken as the structural background against which all visual contents, such as colours, must appear. Examples of the kind to which (4) and (5) belong are, in part, reducible to the extensional logic of relation. To the extent to which they are dependent on linguistic considerations, (4) is based on the statement that "fatherhood" designates a certain irreflexive relation, and (5) on the statement that "to the right of" designates an asymmetrical relation. The conclusion in (4) follows then immediately from the logical property of irreflexive relations that $\sim x R x$; the conclusion in (5) follows from the property of asymmetrical relations that if $x R y$ then $y \breve{R} x$, together with the information that when R is "to the right of", $\breve{R}$ is "to the left of".

The thesis of extensionality is primarily concerned with logical demonstration. In a sense it breaks down in the theory of logic which not only gives a description in connotative terms of what the formulas within an actual demonstration show, but also establishes the conditions of demonstration, among them the conditions of symbolic significance, and thus leads to the doctrine of categories as logical entities which are connotatively distinct from one another. But much as the theory of logic differs from the formalized calculus and much as the difference may remind one of the separation between the metalogic and object-logic, in the intuitional theory there is no real separation because the logical theory is a description of the same thing of which the formulas give an exhibition, viz. of the form of the actual demonstrative thought. For example, the principle that "If one proposition implies another, then the falsehood of the latter implies the falsehood of the former" describes the same thing which is shown by the formula "$p \supset q . \supset . \sim q \supset \sim p$", and both are in their own ways concerned with the form of such concrete statements as "If aggression is provoked by and thus presupposes tolerance of pacifism, then elimination of pacifism would be sufficient to eliminate aggression". And even when in the theory of logic one goes beyond discussions which are descriptive equivalents of symbolic formulas, perhaps beyond statements which could be formalized, the standpoint still remains extensional because however informal the ramifications of a theory may be, they are all ultimately converging upon an explanation of the properties of logical form, which were, to begin with, exhibited for inspection.

Chapter II

THE PARADOXES OF LOGIC

§ 1. INTRODUCTION

Traditional logic places no restriction upon premises which are allowed in deduction unless they are downright contradictions. It is confident that no inconsistency can result in deriving a conclusion in accordance with intuitively certain principles from non-contradictory premises. That is where traditional logic is wrong. Logical paradoxes show inconsistency to be an outcome of certain unrestricted formulations, even when these are seemingly tautological or analytic definitions, i.e. explications of the connotation of some given term. Consistency alone, without regard for the conditions of formation of the premises, is insufficient to insure discourse from contradiction. Modern logic is superior to its traditional predecessor primarily because it has realized the necessity for restrictive conditions of formation, a requirement for the consideration of *significance*. Of course, there has always been an instinctive rejection of certain formations of terms as insignificant; for example, in denouncing "Justice is triangular" as an expression which is neither true nor false but meaningless. Yet this sense for discrimination of significance did not find explicit recognition as a principle among traditional logicians; hence they were helpless in facing logical paradoxes. Russell's

The Problems of Logic

theory of types, as the first systematic treatment of the paradoxes, was a break with tradition and an introduction to logical restrictions of significance.

A basic distinction of significance is between terms or words which are meaningful in isolation and "incomplete symbols" which are merely contributions to meaning and therefore can be understood only in a context. Proper names are examples of isolatable symbols: they stand for individuals or particular presentations. Descriptions (characteristics and relations), on the other hand, are generally contributions to the formation of a propositional structure, the presence of which they outline, but apart from this contribution to a structure they would seem to have no meaning.

"Attributes and relations, though they may be not susceptible of analysis, differ from substances by the fact that they suggest a structure, and that there can be no significant symbol which symbolizes them in isolation. All propositions in which an attribute or a relation *seems* to be the subject are only significant if they can be brought into a form in which the attribute is attributed or the relation relates. If this were not the case, there would be significant propositions in which an attribute or a relation would occupy a position appropriate to a substance, which would be contrary to the doctrine of types. Thus the proper symbol for 'yellow' (assuming for the sake of illustration that this is an attribute) is not the single word 'yellow', but the propositional function 'x is yellow', where the structure of the symbol shows the position which the word 'yellow' must have if it is to be significant."*

The emphasis on significance is a point where Russell breaks completely with the traditional logic of terms; the units of his logic are not single entities, but *propositional functions*, complex expressions of the form "x is ϕ", or, more generally "ϕx", where "x" is the *argument* and "ϕ" the *predicate* (descriptive constituent) of the propositional function. One might think that the notational distinction between the argument and the predicate makes a tacit allowance for the entertainment of the predicate as an isolatable meaning. And one can cite other examples, in which there is an intention to be concerned with characteristics as such rather than with propositional structure. To give one, "I prefer 'green' to 'yellow' " is not intended to mean "I prefer the propositional function 'x is green' to the propositional function 'x is yellow' ". To account for this use of predicates Russell introduces the symbol "$\phi\hat{x}$" (read "phi-ex-cap") which is not a propositional form and therefore, unlike the symbol "ϕx", cannot be transformed into a proposition.† Nevertheless the form "ϕx" remains fundamental in the *Principia* in the sense that it determines the significance of "$\phi \hat{x}$" as well as of any other logical construction, including propositions.

* *Contemporary British Philosophy*, First Series, p. 375. (George Allen & Unwin Ltd.)

† For an illuminating discussion of the purely logical basis of the distinction between these two kinds of function cf. ch. 1 of the mimeographed *Mathematical Logic*, by A. Church.

The Problems of Logic

For a treatment of logical paradoxes the dependence of the significance of propositions on the significance of functions is of primary importance. This dependence can best be explained by introducing the two ways of transformation of a propositional function into a proposition, *evaluation* and *generalization*.

To illustrate these transformations we shall use a propositional function with a fixed meaning, "x is destructible", for which the symbol "fx" will be an *abbreviation*. The process of evaluation is a derivation of a proposition by means of assigning some *value*, i.e. some fixed meaning, to the argument of the function. For example, if we assign to the argument "x" the meaning "Rome", the evaluation gives the proposition *Rome is destructible*, to be abbreviated as "fa".* The same propositional function can also serve as a basis for generalization over the argument, one kind of which gives an existential and another a non-existential proposition, viz. $(\exists x) . fx$,

* The notation used in this book does not differ essentially from the symbolism of the *Principia Mathematica*. But in addition to the convention of using the letters of the beginning of the alphabet as names for individuals and the letters "x", "y", "z" for individual-variables, we shall confine the letters "f", "g", "h" to abbreviations of predicates having a fixed meaning. Such an abbreviation of a proposition as "fa" is to be distinguished from the function "fx" as well as from the function "ϕa", which has a predicate-variable. Without prejudging the question whether a predicate is always a propositional function, we shall use a single letter to designate a predicate as abstracted from its argument. Thus where Russell writes "$\phi \hat{x}$", we shall write instead "ϕ". It is of some interest that in exceptional cases the *Principia* itself adopts this simplified notation. Cf. *Principia Mathematica*, second edition, p. 49.

The Paradoxes of Logic

i.e. *Something is destructible*, and $(x).fx$, i.e. *Everything is destructible*.

A question of consequence for the theory of logical significance is whether or not transformation by generalization can be reduced to transformation by evaluation. Some logicians have tried to identify an existential proposition with a disjunction and a non-existential proposition with a conjunction of singular propositions derivable by evaluation from the same function. According to them "Everything is destructible" means: *Rome is destructible and Mars is destructible and*, etc. (for all values of "*x*"). But in order to identify a general proposition with a collection of singular propositions not only must the latter be actually enumerated but the very possibility of incompleteness of this enumeration should be excluded. This condition is satisfied when either context or perceptual evidence specify the *number* of values which the argument of the propositional function (in the basis of generalization) can take. Let the context be a discussion of probability:

"We throw a single die of normal unbiassed construction under normal conditions. . . . We know (*a*) that the uppermost faces must be either *one* or *two* or *three* or *four* or *five* or *six*, we know (*b*) that it will not be more than one of these."[*]

This context authorizes us to say that "All faces of the die have the same probability of falling uppermost, viz. *1/6*", which means, however, nothing more than the conjunction of singular propositions "The face *one* has the probability (of falling upper-

[*] C. A. Mace, *The Principles of Logic*.

The Problems of Logic

most) *1/6*, and the face *two* has the probability *1/6*, and the face *three* has the probability *1/6*, and the face *four* has the probability *1/6*, and the face *five* has the probability *1/6*, and the face *six* has the probability *1/6*". Instead of a context we sometimes make use of direct perception, as when, entering a room and observing three seats but none of them empty, we say "All seats are occupied", meaning the same as "The first seat is occupied and the second seat is occupied and the third seat is occupied". But, of course, the two statements would not mean the same thing to a person outside the room, to him the conjunction must be conveyed together with the clause of exclusion "And there are no other seats in the room". Without the aid of either perception or context, a general proposition can be reduced to a collection of singular propositions only when the latter are in conjunction with the clause of exclusion "And there are no others" which insures completeness of the enumeration of singular propositions. But the clause of exclusion is itself a general proposition, and therefore our conclusion is that a general proposition as such (i.e. without the aid of additional information from perception or context) is not translatable into singular propositions. This conclusion is strengthened in case the number of singular propositions is too great to be enumerated, or when there are no corresponding singular propositions and the general statement is true vacuously, as is the statement that "All ghosts are transparent".

But while general propositions are irreducible and "generality is seen to be an ultimate mode of signifi-

The Paradoxes of Logic

cance, in extensional logic, where equivalence of propositions is determined exclusively by the identity of their truth-value, the treatment of a general proposition as a truth-function of singular propositions has at least the justification of a fiction useful for computation." A general non-existential proposition would be false when and only when at least one of the singular constituents of the corresponding conjunction is false, and true otherwise. This condition holds even if the number of the constituents should be infinite. And if there are no constituents at all, the condition cannot be violated. *Mutatis mutandis* an analogous condition can be formulated for the reduction of existential propositions.

§ 2. Russell's Theory of Types

Russell's theory of types is a systematic definition of logical significance of propositional functions by means of restrictions put upon the range of values which can be assigned to their arguments.* The *type* of a logical entity is the mode of significance which it takes in a context. Within a propositional function, the simplest kind of context, the type of the function-variable is determined with regard to the possible values of its argument. Thus the signifi-

---

* The following exposition is intended to give the essentials of the doctrine of types without going into such details as the distinctions to be found in the two editions of the *Principia*. I believe these distinctions have now merely an historical interest, for the improvements of the second edition were steps in the direction which has been fully explored since by F. Ramsey. His findings were endorsed later by Russell himself.

The Problems of Logic

cance of "human" in the propositional function "x is human" is its capacity to characterize individuals, where anything that can be tagged by a proper name is an individual. With any other object of characterization the propositional function would be transformed into a meaningless expression. For example, "2 plus 2 is human" is neither true nor false, but insignificant. As a general rule a function cannot significantly take itself as a value. This excludes any such expression as "human is human" or, more generally the form "$\phi \phi$". Given two functions which take the same values of the same kind and therefore are of the same type, neither can be used for reciprocal evaluation. "Proust is famous" and "Proust is human" are both significant; therefore it is meaningless to say either "famous is human" or "human is famous". We can establish now the distinction between the lowest type, the designations of individuals, and the next higher type, the characteristics of individuals.*

But, of course, characteristics of individuals can themselves be described by certain other characteristics. In general, besides functions of individuals there are functions of functions. "Anything human is mortal" is a proposition derived by evaluation from such a function, namely from the expression "Anything ϕ is mortal", which can be written in the abbreviated form "$F \phi$". The function "F" is said

* We do not say "the designations of characteristics of individuals", because in the realist idiom of the *Principia* entities themselves (with the possible exception of individuals), and not merely their symbolic designations, are classified into types of significance.

The Paradoxes of Logic

to be of the next higher type than the function-variable "ϕ" and two types higher than the individual-variable "x". The rule for type-division is very simple: a function is one type higher than the type of its arguments. A systematic application of this rule gives the hierarchy of individuals, functions of individuals, functions of functions of individuals and so on. We can call a function of individuals a function of type 1; a function of functions of individuals a function of type 2; and so on for the succession of higher types.*

In the broad sense of "type", the word is used not only for the divisions of the above hierarchy but also for the distinctions of *order*. We shall always take "type" in its narrow sense, as contrasted with "order". The hierarchy of orders is built up on the basis of a propositional function of any type by means

---

* This hierarchy is sometimes called absolute because it begins with the ontological distinction between individuals and characteristics. But Russell himself has suggested that for all purposes of logic a relative hierarchy, where the type of "individuals" is merely a designation for the lowest type relatively to a context, even if the entities of the lowest type are functions, is sufficient. It is not explained, however, how to determine the rank of types in a context. Suppose we have in a given context three entities of the types "d", "e", "f", respectively. We might decide to take "d" as the type of "individuals", "e" as the type 1, and "f" as the type 2 in a relative hierarchy. But it would seem that unless our decision is purely arbitrary, it must be based on some order established outside the context, in our example, on the order of letters in the alphabet, where "e" comes after "d" and "f" comes after "e". And since the order of the alphabet is not constitutive of the type-significance it must be taken as a symbolic scheme of the absolute hierarchy of types.

The Problems of Logic

of generalization, which means that even when functions have arguments of the same type, they may be functions of different orders. Let us take a function which is a *matrix*, i.e. which is free from generalization, "x is greater than y", or, to abbreviate,

$$g(x, y).$$

By generalizing over either of the variables we derive functions other than matrices:

$$(x) \cdot g(x, y); \; (y) \cdot g(x, y); \; (\exists x) \cdot g(x, y); \; (\exists y) \cdot g(x, y).$$

By generalizing the remaining variable in any of these four expressions we obtain propositions. Thus from the first expression we derive:

$$(x)(y) \cdot g(x, y); \; (x)(\exists y) \cdot g(x, y).$$

The original matrix as well as all the derivative expressions and propositions belong to the first order. A logical entity of the first order contains only individual-variables, free or bound. From this definition it follows that a truth-function, of which the constituents are expressions of the first order, is itself a first-order expression. To have a second-order function we must take a matrix in which both the predicate and the argument are variables; we separate the predicate from the argument by an exclamation sign to indicate that the symbol is a matrix:

$$\phi \, ! \, x \text{ (read "phi-shriek-ex")}.$$

Let this be a function of two variables, "ϕ" and

The Paradoxes of Logic

"x", where the values of "ϕ" are first-order functions, such as "destructible", "greater than", etc. Then the matrix "$\phi \,!\, x$", as well as any expression or proposition derived from it by generalization, is a logical entity of the second order. To understand the significance of the distinction between characteristics of the first and the second order, let us examine the expression:

x has all the characteristics of an artist.

"Having all the characteristics of an artist" is itself a characteristic of an artist, but in a new sense which was not meant in the original meaning of the word "characteristic"; in the new sense it is a function of the second order, originally it was taken as a function of the first order. We have here an illustration of the difference between the forms "$(\phi) \,.\, \phi\, x$" and "$f\, x$". Both are functions of "x", and the first form can be written as "$F(\phi, x)$", but a restriction of order-significance allows for "f" while it excludes "F" as a possible value of "ϕ" in the matrix "$\phi \,!\, x$". As we have here a distinction between first-order and second-order functions, so we can proceed further with the recognition of functions of still higher orders. The rule that a function-variable can take as values only functions of a lower order than itself determines the clear-cut separation of one order from another.

The hierarchy of types (in the narrow sense) together with the hierarchies of order within each type form the so-called *branched* division of types (in the broad sense). The subsequent developments

The Problems of Logic

of the theory of logical significance have, in the main, consisted in efforts to abolish the distinctions of order and to retain only the *simple hierarchy* in which the type of a function is determined by the type of its argument.*

§ 3. The Paradoxes

The paradoxes can be divided into two groups: the logical paradoxes which are resolved by the divisions of type and the epistemological paradoxes which can be dealt with by means of the distinctions of order.

The most famous example of the first group is Russell's paradox of the class of classes which are not members of themselves. In order to avoid the misconception that this paradox is merely a disclosure of an inherent inconsistency in the notion of a class, it is advisable to formulate it in the language of propositional functions.

Functions either can or cannot be predicated of themselves. "Conceivable" is itself a conceivable characteristic. But the property "feline", unlike a

---

* Even among the recent expositors of the doctrine of types the basic importance of the distinction between types and orders has not always been understood. Thus the account in *Symbolic Logic* by C. I. Lewis and C. H. Langford is virtually worthless because of the insufficient statement on p. 454: "Thus functions of different orders are necessarily of different types, whereas functions of the same order may or may not be of the same type. However, not much emphasis is placed upon this difference of type within the same order, and for all practical purposes functions of the same order can be regarded as being of the same type."

The Paradoxes of Logic

cat, is not itself feline. A function or characteristic which is not predicable of itself may be called impredicable and symbolized by "I". The formularized definition of I is:

$$I(\phi) = \sim \phi(\phi) \text{ . Def.}$$

This definition allows for the equivalence:

$$(\phi) \text{ . } I(\phi) \equiv \sim \phi(\phi).$$

Since the equivalence is true for every ϕ, it must be true when ϕ is given the value I:

$$I(I) \equiv \sim I(I).$$

But this result is a contradiction.

Resolution: The simple hierarchy of types rules out any expression in which a function is an argument of itself. Hence the formularized definition of I, in the definiens of which ϕ is the argument of ϕ, must be rejected as meaningless.

The epistemological paradoxes were already known to the ancient Greeks in the form of Epimenides' predicament.

Epimenides, who was a Cretan himself, is supposed to have said that "All Cretans are liars". If we interpret his statement as "All Cretan assertions are false" and *assume*, for the sake of argument, that all other Cretan statements actually were false, then Epimenides' own statement leads to a contradiction. For if it were true, according to its own meaning it should be false along with other Cretan assertions. And if it were false, then there should be some true

The Problems of Logic

Cretan statement, in fact it should be Epimenides' own statement since by assumption the other Cretan statements could not be true. And so "the music goes round and round". Let us formularize the argument. We shall use "s" as a statement-variable, "e" as a name for Epimenides' assertion, "f" as an abbreviation for the characteristic "asserted by Cretans".

(1) $\sim(\exists s).[fs.s.\sim(s=e)]$.   By assumption
(2) $e. \equiv [(s).(fs \supset \sim s)]$.   By definition of e
(3) $e \supset (fe \supset \sim e)$.   By (2)
(4) $[(fe \supset \sim e).fe] \supset \sim e$.   By the principle that "$[(p \supset q).p] \supset q$"
(5) fe.   By information
(6) $e \supset \sim e$.   By (3), (4), & (5)
(7) $\sim e \supset [(\exists s).(fs.s)]$ By (2)
(8) $\sim e \supset e$.   By (1) and (7)
(9) $e \equiv \sim e$.   By (6) and (8)

The division of propositions into orders gives an easy solution of the difficulty. Epimenides' assertion, if intended to apply to itself, is meaningless. It can be interpreted as a meaningful statement only if it is one order higher than the Cretan propositions it refers to. But if so, the transition from (2) to (3), whereby s takes e as a value, is illegitimate. And without this transition there is no contradiction.

Even a more striking epistemological paradox, usually taken to be merely a simplified version of "Epimenides", is the assertion "I am lying" or

The Paradoxes of Logic

"This proposition is false" (when it is intended to apply to itself). Grelling's thorough analysis of it, for which he himself gives credit to Lukasiewicz, is as follows.*

"Let 'q' be an abbreviation of the phrase 'the proposition on the 8th line of this page'. Then let us write:

(1) *q is a false proposition.*

By counting the lines we verify:

(2) *q is identical with the proposition (1).*

(3) *q is a false proposition* is equivalent to non-q.†

The first member of this equivalence (printed in italics) is our proposition (1). Thus we have:

(4) The proposition (1) is equivalent to non-q.

But in virtue of (2) *the proposition* (1) can be replaced by q. Thus results the contradiction:

(5) q is equivalent to non-q."

In order to solve this paradox, we observe that if we give to q in (1) its value in accordance with (2), we can rewrite (1) as: (1) The proposition (1) is a false proposition.

But if this were a proposition it would mean a violation of the order-prohibition of general propositions (and a singular proposition involving a definite description is a species of a general pro-

* Cf. K. Grelling, "The Logical Paradoxes", *Mind*, 1936.
† This equivalence is assumed to be generally accepted in logic.

position) which apply to themselves. Hence expression (1) is meaningless and not a proposition.

The foregoing exposition conforms with Russell's original view that the same "vicious-circle" principle, which outlaws the application of an expression to itself, resolves both the logical and the epistemological paradoxes:

"Whatever involves *all* of a collection must not be one of the collection; or, conversely: If, provided a certain collection had a total, it would have members only definable in terms of that total, then the said collection has no total."[*]

But Russell's own disciple, F. Ramsey, has shown that the difference between the logical and the epistemological paradoxes is so essential that they require different treatment. He also raised some doubts about the "vicious-circle" principles, which have been fully justified by recent developments in the formalist logic: there are legitimate expressions which are about themselves.

§ 4. CRITICISM OF THE ORDER-HIERARCHY

The main fault with the hierarchy of orders is that it rules out, together with the epistemological paradoxes, certain important propositions which otherwise would seem to be perfectly correct.

A traditional philosophical method of refuting a thesis is by showing that it cannot stand its own test. When the sceptic tells us that nothing can be known,

---

[*] Russell and Whitehead, *Principia Mathematica*, second edition, p. 39.

The Paradoxes of Logic

the philosopher answers that if this were so, the sceptic could not know it to be so. Such an answer is effective and philosophers would hate to give it up merely because according to the doctrine of orders no thesis can be self-refuting since no proposition can be about itself.

Yet in the movement against the order-hierarchy it was not philosophers but mathematicians who took the lead. They did it in defence of an important kind of mathematical procedure, which is exemplified in the definition of the least upper bound of a series of real numbers.

The least upper bound of a set of numbers in the ascending order of magnitude is the least number which is not less than any number in the set. If among the numbers of the set there is one which is the greatest, it is called the *maximum*, and, in this case, it is the least upper bound. For example, in the series "1, 2, 3, 4, 5" the upper bound and the maximum is 5. On the other hand, when there is no greatest number in the set, the least upper bound is a certain number outside the set. In the dense series of all rational fractions less than 1, the upper bound is its limit 1, which is the least number of a series of rationals from 1 upward. Now according to Dedekind's postulate, if we divide any ascending series of numbers into two jointly exhaustive and mutually exclusive series, the lower section and the upper section, then there is a dividing number which is the upper bound of the lower section. But it would seem that the series of rationals does not satisfy Dedekind's postulate. For suppose we divide this

The Problems of Logic

series into the lower section of all fractions whose square is less than 2 and the upper section of all fractions whose square is greater than 2. Since it can be proved that there exists no fraction the square of which is equal to 2, there is no number which divides the sections unless, to save the postulate, we construct a pure fiction, the existence of the irrational $\sqrt{2}$ as the dividing number. However, there is a better procedure than indulgence in fictions; the series of rationals can be transformed into a new series, which satisfies Dedekind's requirement, the continuous series of positive *real numbers*. The terms of this series are not the rationals themselves but *classes* of positive rationals, and the ascending series of these classes is ordered by the relation of whole and part. To build up this derivative series we define its terms as classes of positive rationals which have no maximum in the original series of rationals. This means that to every rational number there corresponds a term of the derivative. Corresponding to $\frac{1}{2}$ there is "the class of fractions smaller than $\frac{1}{2}$", corresponding to the rational 1 "the class of proper fractions"; and so on. But the derivative series of real numbers also contains terms to which there is no corresponding fraction; one of these terms is "the class of all rationals smaller than $\sqrt{2}$", and it is identified with $\sqrt{2}$. Clearly $\sqrt{2}$ is the least upper bound of all those classes of rationals that correspond to rationals whose square is less than 2. In general an upper bound of a series of real numbers is defined as the real number which is the logical

The Paradoxes of Logic

sum of the real numbers smaller than it. In other words, the members of the upper bound are all those rationals which are members of any class-term of the series concerned. In the language of propositional functions or characteristics we can say that the membership of the upper bound is defined by the characteristic of "having any of the characteristics which determine the membership of those classes which are the terms of the series". But according to the divisions of order the characteristic of having any of the characteristics (of a kind) is of a higher order than the latter. Thus if the latter define real numbers, the former, being higher in order, cannot be a real number. And there the theory of real numbers breaks down.

In order to counteract this adverse effect of the hierarchy of orders Russell offered his *Axiom of Reducibility*:

$$(\exists \psi).(\phi x \equiv \psi! x),$$ i.e.

Given a function of any order ϕ, there exists an equivalent function of the first order ψ, where "equivalent" means that with the same values of the arguments both functions are transformed into propositions which have the same truth-value. With the aid of the Axiom of Reducibility the characteristic of having any characteristic which determines the membership of the class-terms of a series of real numbers can be replaced in the definition of the upper bound by an equivalent characteristic one order lower, and when the upper bound of a series of real numbers is thus redefined it itself can be

The Problems of Logic

taken as a real number. This saves the mathematical theory, but raises the question of justification of the Axiom of Reducibility.

There is no doubt that in ordinary language we have no difficulty in reducing the order of characteristics. The characteristic of having any characteristic of an artist is, perhaps, equivalent to the characteristic of a lower order "temperamental" or "observant" or, if this is not so, to a disjunction of first-order characteristics that artists have ever had. A further evidence in favour of the Axiom, at least for those logicians who believe in the existence of classes, is that their belief entails the Axiom, as Russell himself has pointed out. If there are classes, then a function of any order "ϕx" determines a class "C" of those values of the argument of the function which transform the latter into a true proposition. Then we can say "x is a member of C". But this expression is equivalent to "ϕx" and is itself a first-order function.

Sometimes a fear is voiced that the Axiom of Reducibility is in effect a removal of all barriers of type and order, a removal which is at the same time a restoration of the contradictions. This is not so. The Axiom of Reducibility does not affect the simple hierarchy of types, because it is concerned with the reduction of order exclusively. Nor does it reinstate the epistemological paradoxes; for the cause of these is not a mere confusion in taking functions of different orders to be equivalent with respect to their truth-value, but rather the practice of substituting one function for another with no contextual

The Paradoxes of Logic

restriction and in disregard of their difference in connotation. As Ramsey puts it:

". . . this second set of contradictions are not purely mathematical, but all involve the ideas of thought or meaning, in connection with which equivalent functions (in the sense of equivalent explained above) are not interchangeable; for instance, one can be meant by a certain word or symbol, but not the other, and one can be definable, and not the other."*

There remains a general objection, and Ramsey makes much of it, that the Axiom of Reducibility is not an analytic truth or a tautology. This objection may have weight with the members of the logistic school, who want only indubitable principles as a basis for logic, but it should be irrelevant so far as the postulationalists are concerned since they have no regard for axiomatic self-evidence and can accept without scruples the Axiom of Reducibility as one postulate among others.

It is undeniable, however, that the whole construction of the order-hierarchy together with its annex, the Axiom of Reducibility, is extremely cumbersome. Even without the Axiom, one must put up with the awkward condition of an endless duplication, for every order of the hierarchy, of the set of logical principles. For instance let the principle be:

$$(p) \cdot (p \lor \sim p).$$

According to the doctrine of orders this principle

* F. Ramsey, *The Foundations of Mathematics*, p. 28, Kegan Paul, 1931.

The Problems of Logic

cannot apply to itself. Yet it must be either true or false. Hence we must either subsume it under another principle of the excluded middle, of a higher order, or else, which is much simpler, try to do away with the orders altogether.

§ 5. Rejection of Order-Divisions

The abolishment of the hierarchy of orders is the result of Ramsey's work. He knew that order-ascension depends on generalization, he also knew that in extensional logic general propositions have the same significance as truth-functions of singular propositions; the conclusion that there is no logical significance in the divisions of order was inevitable.

Ramsey's critics, who believe that he overlooked the difference in connotation between a general proposition and the corresponding combination of singular propositions, are entirely wrong. Not only he did not overlook this difference, but, on the contrary, he used it as a guiding principle in his solution of the epistemological paradoxes, which is as follows.

Whatever the relation between a general proposition and the corresponding truth-function, they differ in *formulation*. By means of such linguistic differences one can express different *ways of meaning* things, even when the things referred to are the same. Let two distinct formulas F_1 and F_2 express two different relations of meaning M_1 and M_2, the object of reference being in both cases O, and

The Paradoxes of Logic

"$M(F, O)$" be an abbreviation of "The formula F means by the relation of meaning M the object meant O". Then, it is clear that while "$M_1(F_1, O)$" and "$M_2(F_2, O)$" are true, "$M_1(F_2, O)$" and "$M_2(F_1, O)$" are false. These symbolic illustrations show that a misuse of the relation of meaning generates *falsehood* and not lack of significance. Ramsey concludes that the epistemological paradoxes are instances of such a misuse of meaning and therefore result in falsehood. For example, Epimenides the Cretan must have meant, in a sense which can be called M_2, that "All propositions meant (in a sense to be called M_1) by Cretans are false". There is no paradox unless one confuses M_2 with M_1. But this confusion does not transgress logical significance, it is simply a false description of how Epimenides meant what he said.*

Of course, M_2 may be said to be a higher order of meaning than M_1, and since this would lead to a hierarchy of orders of meaning, the corresponding propositions must also be arranged in a hierarchy of orders. In fact, this gives the same hierarchy as Russell's, with the important difference that it represents variation in formulation and not distinctions in logical form.

"My solutions of these contradictions," says Ramsey, "are obviously very similar to those of Whitehead and Russell, the difference between them lying merely in our different conceptions of the

* This is merely a brief summary of the involved argument to be found in the op. cit., pp. 42–49.

The Problems of Logic

order of propositions and functions. For me, propositions in themselves have no orders; they are just different truth-functions of atomic propositions—a definite totality, depending only on what atomic propositions there are. Orders and illegitimate totalities only come in with the symbols we use to symbolize the facts in various complicated ways."[*] Ramsey's rejection of order-divisions was accepted almost universally and logicians have concentrated in subsequent writing upon the simple hierarchy of types. The work of the postulationalists has been, in this respect, especially impressive. But I think that the intuitionalist has the right to point out that Ramsey's argument is conclusive only within the logic of propositions. When the elements of logic are merely sentences or strings of marks, the distinctions between the different ways of meaning cannot be made. Of course, this distinction is unnecessary for a postulational system taken in abstraction from its interpretations. The question, however, must be raised whether metalogic or semantics which refer to the object-logic should take account of the various ways of reference. And if it should, one might expect that rejection of propositions as distinct from mere sentences must force the postulationalists to recognize the various ways of reference as so many different *logical* formulations. This would be, in effect, giving up Ramsey's conclusion that the divisions of order have no logical significance.

[*] Op. cit., p. 48 f.

The Paradoxes of Logic

§ 6. The Postulational Treatment of Types

There is a sharp distinction between the principles of consistency and significance in logistic; even the grounds of their assertion are not the same; the rules of significance are not intuitively certain, they have the air of *ad hoc* devices to escape from the logical paradoxes.

The postulational logic has the advantage of a uniform treatment; since it has no regard for intuitive self-evidence, it can formulate the restrictions of significance in the same way in which it gives the other initial conditions of procedure as so many postulates. Thus it might profit from Russell's simple hierarchy of types by postulating it and then annexing to the other postulates of its system. Such a simple procedure would be advisable, if it were not for the fact that, even when purged from the complications of order, the theory of types is far from being satisfactory. The defects of the simple theory of types are ably summed up in a statement by W. V. Quine:

"But the theory of types has unnatural and inconvenient consequences. Because the theory allows a class to have members only of uniform type, the universal class V gives way to an infinite series of quasi-universal classes, one for each type. The negation $-x$ ceases to comprise all non-members of x, and comes to comprise only those non-members of x which are next lower in type than x. Even the null-class gives way to an infinite series of null classes. The Boolean class algebra no longer applies to classes

The Problems of Logic

in general, but is reproduced rather within each type. The same is true of the calculus of relations. Even arithmetic, when introduced by definitions on the basis of logic, proves to be subject to the same reduplication. Thus the numbers cease to be unique; a new *0* appears for each type, likewise a new *1*, and so on, just as in the case of V and ∧. Not only are all these cleavages and reduplications intuitively repugnant, but they call continually for more or less elaborate technical manœuvres by way of restoring severed connections."*

This criticism raises a two-fold problem. On the one hand, since the hierarchy of types leads to "unnatural and inconvenient consequences", it must be dispensed with. On the other hand, formations of symbols which lead to paradoxes must be ruled out without the aid of type-divisions. The postulational logic has all the technical equipment for the solution of this problem. It rejects the restrictions of type by allowing a function to be its own argument. With this allowance there are at least three methods of avoiding the paradoxes, associated in American literature with the names of Alonzo Church, W. V. Quine, and H. Curry, respectively.†

* "New Foundations for Mathematical Logic," p. 78 f. *Am. Math. Monthly*, February 1937.

† In the following sketch no attempt is made to be faithful to the rigour and thoroughness of the original presentations, for which the reader is referred to *Mathematical Logic*, Lectures by Alonzo Church, Princeton University, 1935–36, pp. 16 ff.; *New Foundations for Mathematics*, by W. V. Quine, pp. 77 ff.; and "First Properties of Functionality in Combinatory Logic", by H. B. Curry, *The Tohoku Mathematical Journal*, February 1936.

The Paradoxes of Logic

Church offers a definite criterion for dividing expressions into two groups. He defines one of them as the group of meaningless expressions and shows that it contains the logical paradoxes.

In his system symbolic expressions bracketed after the pattern

(1) $$[---](\ldots)$$

indicate that it is permissible to substitute for the free variable of the function within the square brackets the whole expression in round brackets. The rules of substitution are formalized and their application may or may not terminate in a derivative formula without free variables. If it does, the original formula is said to be meaningful, otherwise it is meaningless. There are no postulates which would rule out as insignificant such a formula as "$\sim \phi(\phi)$", where ϕ is an argument to itself. But take

(2) $$[\sim \phi(\phi)](\sim \phi(\phi)).$$

This expression is bracketed after the pattern (1) and therefore in agreement with the rules of substitutions can be transformed into

(3) $$\sim [\sim \phi(\phi)](\sim \phi(\phi)).$$

But (3) shows the same pattern of bracketing as in (1); and the corresponding substitution leads back to (2). This circle is an expression of Russell's paradox, but (2) is now rejected by definition of a meaningless formula, and not because it involves a function which is applied to itself.

In Quine's procedure, his observation that only one rule of the system can be responsible for the occurrence of Russell's paradox makes him postulate a restriction upon substitution for the free variables involved in this rule, while all other rules remain free from restrictions.

Quine shows that Russell's paradox in the form

$$(\exists x) . [(x \in x) \equiv \sim (x \in x)]$$

is a special case of the theorem

$$(\exists x)(Y) . [(Y \in x) \equiv \sim (Y \in Y)],$$

which can be derived in his system by the rule $R\ 3$: If "x" does not occur in ϕ, $(x)(Y):(Y \in x) \equiv \phi$ is a theorem. The introduction of a restriction is said to *stratify* ϕ, but only within the context of $R\ 3$. In accordance with stratification, whenever ϕ is a complex involving the relationship of membership ϵ, the variable on the left of ϵ must be one type lower (using the terminology of the theory of types) than the type of the variable on the right side. To quote Quine:

"I will now suggest a method of avoiding the contradictions without accepting the theory of types or the disagreeable consequence which it entails. Whereas the theory of types avoids the contradictions by excluding unstratified formulas from the language altogether, we might gain the same end by continuing to countenance unstratified formulas. Under this method we abandon the hier-

The Paradoxes of Logic

archy of types, and think of the variables as unrestricted in range. But the notion of stratified formula ... survives at one point: we replace $R\ 3$ by the weaker rule:

$R\ 3'$. If ϕ is stratified and does not contain 'x', $(\exists\ x)(\Upsilon)(\Upsilon \in x) \equiv \phi)$ is a theorem."*

Finally, Curry offers a formal method for determining the logical categories of various expressions. A function applied to itself—which can be written in Curry's simplified notation of rows of entities as ff—gives rise to Russell's paradox only if it comes under the category of a proposition, but nothing in the rules of his system indicate that it should be so interpreted.

Curry shows that the form of Russell's paradox

$$ff = \sim (ff)$$

can be proved in his system by a joint use of the operators W and B. A row of two entities prefixed by W give the original row with the last entity duplicated. Thus

(1) $\qquad W(B\ N)f = B\ Nff.$

The result of prefixing a row of three entities by B, is the bracketing of the last two entities of the row as a single expression.

(2) $\qquad B\ Nff = N(ff).$

Since f and N may be anything, let f be defined as

* Op. cit., p. 79.

WBN and N as the sign of negation "$\sim$". These definitions transform (1) and (2) into

$$ff = B \sim ff;$$
$$B \sim ff = \sim (ff),$$

from which it follows that

$$ff = \sim (ff).$$

Curry then shows that in his system ff may not be a proposition and therefore the last equation is not a contradiction.

All three methods seem to be formally correct. This however, cannot be ascertained before it is proved that they do not lead to inconsistency within and in conjunction with the postulational systems to which they belong. Thus in the postulational logic the problem of significance becomes an aspect of the problem of consistency. Negatively this is shown in all three methods sketched above since they have no use for the distinctions of type-significance and allow a function to take itself as a value of its argument. Positively the tendency to disregard significance (as distinct from consistency) by making it a matter of interpretation is most pronounced in Curry's procedure. But while the tendency to reduce logical difficulties to questions of consistency can be praised as leading to basic simplification, so far as the paradoxes are concerned it means a postponement of their solution. First, because the solution must wait for the proof of the consistency of the system; secondly, because the proofs of consistency

The Paradoxes of Logic

are metalogical discussions in which reference to certain formulas of the object-system revives the epistemological paradoxes. And since the postulationalists cannot resort to Ramsey's mere linguistic distinctions of order as opposed to distinctions of significance, they end by making a much more drastic distinction of languages which are irreducible to one another. Thus, according to Gödel, any language B, however rich, cannot contain such expressions as "false statement in B"; these expressions must belong to a meta-language. But surely one does talk in English about "false English statements". The postulationalists declare that this proves that English is self-contradictory! To my mind to say that English is self-contradictory is to indulge in a paradox far more intolerable than "Epimenides" or any other epistemological puzzle; it certainly is not giving a solution of the puzzles.

§ 7. An Individual Examination of the Paradoxes

The strength of the postulational logic—the explicit statement and formularization of all the postulates and rules in use in the system—is more likely than anything else to be in the long run a weakness in its dealing with the paradoxes. For, as a fixed set the postulates of a system may be too rigid, even if they have disposed of all difficulties up to date, to meet the emergency of some new puzzle or even of some original version of an old one. After all Ramsey made a step forward when he understood that there is no single principle, such as

The Problems of Logic

Russell's "vicious-circle" principle, which would do away with all logical difficulties. But perhaps his own division of paradoxes into two groups was still too summary as a way for complete success. And if so, it would seem to be profitable to relinquish any set-up mechanism, but approach the paradoxes individually, as they come out, and without the prejudice that the method of dealing with one of them would be effective with another. Accordingly and in contrast with the postulationists who operate with a fixed number, however great, of rules, I shall examine each paradox with the possibility in mind that it might require a unique treatment or even suggest the formulation of a principle which has never been thought of before. Of course, this attitude marks a belief in the flexibility and resourcefulness of logical intuition.

I shall begin with my own version of the "Epimenides" which is so formulated as not to be amenable to the kinds of solution which are given by either Russell or Ramsey.

> All propositions written within the rectangle of Fig. 1 are false.

Fig. 1

Let the expression within the rectangle of Fig. 1 be called a and let f denote the phrase "written within the rectangle of Fig. 1." Then:

The Paradoxes of Logic

(1) $\quad fa,$

(2) $\quad \sim (\exists p) \cdot [fp \cdot \sim (p = a)].$

(3) $\quad a = (p) \cdot (fp \supset \sim p).$

Suppose a is itself a proposition. Then if a is true:

$$fa \supset \sim a, \quad \text{by (3)}$$
$$\underline{fa\phantom{\supset \sim a, \quad \text{by (3)}}}$$

(4) $\qquad\qquad\qquad \sim a$

But if $\sim a$, then (3) gives:

$$(\exists p) \cdot (fp \cdot p).$$

This result is compatible with (2) only if:

(5) $\qquad\qquad\qquad a.$

The vicious circle—from (4) to (5) and back—cannot be avoided if, following Russell, we declare that a, intended to apply to itself, is not a proposition but a meaningless expression. If a is not a proposition, then:

$$\sim (\exists p) \cdot fp, \quad \text{by (2)}.$$

This means that there are no propositions at all within the rectangle of Fig. 1. But then there are no true propositions there either:

(6) $\qquad\qquad \sim (\exists p) \cdot (fp \cdot p).$

But (6) is another formulation of "$(p) \cdot fp \supset \sim p$" which by (3) is equal to a. Therefore a is true. But if a is true, it must be a proposition, assuming in agreement with ordinary logic that nothing but a proposition can be true. Thus if *a* is not a proposition, it is a proposition and *vice versa*. This is again a circle in argument which is just as bad as the vacillation between (4) and (5). Thus Russell's treatment cannot resolve the paradox of Fig. I.*

* A reviewer of my version of the "Epimenides", C. H. Langford, decided that it does not differ "relevantly" from the original paradox (*The Journal of Symbolic Logic*, vol. 3, No. 1, 1938). His decision comes from a lack of understanding of my version as well as of the usual (i.e. Russell's) solution of the paradoxes. According to the reviewer, "It is not the case that the usual resolution of the paradox Ushenko cites is to the effect that the sentence within Fig. I is meaningless. . . . On the usual view, the sentence in question expresses a second-order proposition. . . ." But even if *a* could be reinterpreted as a second-order proposition, in its original interpretation, when it was intended (as it was in my exposition) to be about itself, it would have to be ruled out, on the usual view, as meaningless. However the important point, which the reviewer did not see, is that a reinterpretation of *a* as a second-order proposition is impossible, because a second-order proposition must be about first-order propositions, whereas *a* is not about first-order propositions; *a* is about propositions within the rectangle of Fig. I, and since, with the possible exception of *a* itself, there are no propositions there there are no first-order propositions there either. The reviewer should keep in mind Russell's own words: "It is important to observe that, since there are various types of propositions and functions . . . all phrases referring to 'all propositions' or 'all functions', or to 'some (undetermined) proposition' or 'some (undetermined) function' are *prima facie* meaningless, though in certain cases they are capable of an unobjectionable interpretation." (Op. cit., p. 166.) Professor Church has criticized my argument from a standpoint which is opposite to that of Mr. Langford, viz. he thinks that the statement *a* is meaningless because it contains the phrase "all propositions" without an indication of their order. But an indication of the order is not necessary if the phrase refers to a well-defined class of propositions, each of these being of a determinate order, as when

The Paradoxes of Logic

Nor would Ramsey's distinction of different "ways of meaning" be of any help here. For the expression *a* involves "writing" instead of "meaning", it is written within a rectangle and is itself about propositions written within a rectangle; and "writing", unlike "meaning", has no different senses which might lead to confusion or falsehood.*

A very simple resolution of this paradox would be a demonstration that it is not a paradox but a downright contradiction. Of course, the paradox leads to a contradiction when its implications are made explicit, but it remains a paradox so long as it appears that its formation agrees with the principles of logical significance while its descriptive import is an empirical fact as given by Fig. I. On the other hand, there would be no paradox if one could show that *a* violates the principles of logical formation and

we say that "All propositions on p. 1 of this book are either true or false". The sentence *a* is not about all propositions without restriction, but about "all-propositions-within-the-rectangle-of-Fig. I"; the hyphened expression may stand for a null class, but a null class is a well-defined class.

* There might be a concealed reference to "meaning" in *a*, if as Professor Church pointed out to me, we must assume that only sentences and not propositions can be written and therefore take *a* as a sentence which *means* a proposition. This objection, it seems to me, is of an epistemological order. On purely logical grounds the question whether or not a proposition can be written remains open. So far as my own epistemological stand is concerned I believe that a proposition is "embodied" in a sentence, so that the former is written down along with the latter. Even if a proposition were a universal of which the corresponding sentences are instances, it would be present literally, as a whole, in each of its exemplifying instances.

because of this violation is a concealed expression of "$p \cdot \sim p$". Accordingly, I suggest that *a* is not a paradox because it contradicts itself by contradicting the principle of logical significance which belongs to any proposition-form, viz., the "claim to truth". In its usual symbolic formulation this principle is given as an equivalence:

$$p \equiv (p = 1).$$

Should *p* assert its own falsehood, it would assert that "$p = 0$" and the equivalence would be transformed into:

$$p \equiv (0 = 1),$$

which is a contradiction. Thus we must reject *a*, which asserts its own falsehood, not as a paradox but as an outright contraction of the form "$0 = 1$" or "$p \cdot \sim p$". Indeed, since *a* has an implicit claim to truth, it can be given explicitly as the conjunction:

a. the proposition expressed by "*a*" is true.

But in virtue of its meaning which is intended to apply to itself, *a* can be replaced in the conjunction by the weaker constituent:

The proposition expressed by "*a*" is false.

The result gives the contradiction:

The proposition expressed by "*a*" is false. The proposition expressed by ""*a* is true.

It is easy to show that the same principle can be applied to the original "Epimenides" and, in general, to any expression of the form:

The Paradoxes of Logic

All propositions of the kind, of which this is one, are false.

But I think a different treatment is required for the singular form:

(*a*)   This proposition is false.

The difficulty here does not depend on self-attribution of falsehood, since a similar difficulty, and infinite regress, is found in the form:

(*b*)   This proposition is true.

Hence the singular form (*a*) is not a mere variation of the "Epimenides", and must be referred to some different principle which could also solve the difficulty of (*b*). Such a new solution is found in the observation that (*a*) and (*b*), when intended to apply to themselves are not propositions but propositional functions, whose evaluation would always give falsehood.

Take the form (*a*). Since it is intended to be a statement about itself, it can be expressed as:

(*a*) is false,

where (*a*) is supposed to name the whole expression. But no sign can name (or single out) an object whose constitution involves that very sign, therefore (*a*) must be a pseudo-name, in fact it is nothing but a variable. And if (*a*) is a variable, then the expression "(*a*) is false" must be a propositional function whose substitution for (*a*) would be a statement about a proposition function, viz.:

"(*a*) is false" is false,

which is false or meaningless because a propositional

The Problems of Logic

function cannot be false. If one tried to avoid the use of a pseudo-name by interpreting "this" in "this proposition is false" not as a demonstrative symbol but as a description of "the proposition under consideration", one would miss directness of reference with a resulting ambiguity, and, which is worse, one would violate a distinction of significance by confusing a description of a proposition with the proposition itself. For to say that the phrase "the proposition (a)" means the same as "the proposition (a) is false" is to identify a description with a would-be proposition of which the former is a constituent. Some such confusion I find in Grelling's version given on p. 49, where "q" is first introduced not as a name of a proposition, but as an abbreviation of the definite description "the proposition on the 13th line of p. 49," and later identified with (1), although (1) is advanced as a proposition and not as a descriptive phrase.

But even if consistency alone were the right tool to work with the epistemological paradoxes, recourse to *significance* must be made when we come to Russell's "class of classes which are not members of themselves." Only I think that Russell is too summary when he asserts that all attributes indicate a structure. Let us try to discriminate. For example, we may compare the attributes "conceivable" and "yellow". Certainly "conceivable" means "an object of conception" and this phrase is a structure. But "yellow" can be visualized, and therefore thought of, in isolation from, i.e. without imagining it together with, a particular object. The evidence of

The Paradoxes of Logic

this example suggests a division of predicates into two groups: the predicates which are and the predicates which are not propositional functions. Of course, such a division if actually carried out, would depend on the connotation of predicates, but in abstraction from connotation it can be taken as a restrictive condition of logical formation to the effect that a predicate which is a structure or a propositional function cannot take another such predicate as a value of its argument. If $f(x)$ is a propositional function and g is a predicate without a structure, $f(g)$ is significant (unless further consideration of connotation rules it out), but $f(fx)$ is not. This condition excludes Russell's paradox. Let us take the attribute "Impredicable". This is a propositional function to which we have already attached the symbol:

$$I(x).$$

In conformity with the restrictive condition of significance the argument x of this function must take its values within the range of attributes which, like "yellow", have no structure. Hence "Impredicable" cannot be predicated of itself. The expressions "I (I)" and "$\sim$ I (I)" are illegitimate because they are short for the forms:

$$I(Ix); \sim I(Ix),$$

which the restrictive condition rules out.

The paradoxes of logic have had a long and vexatious history, and I would not be surprised if my own resolutions will be found faulty. But the method of individual treatment always allows for a

The Problems of Logic

re-examination. Also logical intuition shows an almost unlimited ingenuity. A failure of a postulational system to deal with the paradoxes would be equivalent to a condemnation of the system. But if intuition has so far failed, we can say that we have not yet discovered the intuitive principle which is relevant to the problem.

Chapter III

CONSISTENCY AND THE DECISION-PROBLEM

§ 1. INTRODUCTION

The problem of consistency is a peculiarity of the postulational logic. When the principles of logic are accepted on purely intuitive grounds, there can be no question concerning their truth and significance. And if they are both true and significant, they cannot lead to inconsistency. Even in the semi-postulational procedure of logistic there is no need for a proof of consistency. Once the theory of types is introduced in order to insure significance, the primitive propositions of a logistic system are known to be mutually consistent because they are recognized to be true by immediate inspection. In a postulational system of logic, on the other hand, the restrictions of significance are not derived from ontological distinctions; they are incorporated into the arbitrary rules of procedure. The starting-point of the procedure is formed by the postulates which, like the rules, are also accepted by convention. Under these circumstances it is always possible to expect, unless a proof to the contrary is given, the emergence of a paradox, which was not anticipated when the conventions were introduced, or of a contradiction, which would disclose that some conventions in the basis of the system happen to clash with others. But

The Problems of Logic

within the system the demonstration of theorems may have gone a long way before one stumbles against inconsistency. Obviously one wants to find the weakness of the foundation not by means of the collapse of the building but before one has started to build. For this reason the question whether the postulational system is contradictory must be decided by theoretical (or metalogical) considerations and not through the procedure carried on within the system.

A proof of consistency is a demonstration that with the postulates and rules of the formal system no two theorems can be deduced which contradict one another. Thus to prove that the calculus of unanalysed propositions, i.e. the calculus whose variables, p, q, etc., are interpretable as propositions, is consistent, one must show that p and $\sim p$ are not both theorems. As explained in § 2, if both p and $\sim p$ are deducible, then any formula q is deducible or is a theorem. Conversely, if a system contains a formula which is not a theorem, the system must be consistent. The presence of unprovable formulas might be suggested as a practical criterion of consistency, provided one could always decide whether a given formula is provable or not. But the possibility of such a decision is itself a problem, known as the "*decision-problem*" (Entscheidung problem). The question is whether there exists, with regard to any given formula of a postulational system of logic, a finite procedure, i.e. a procedure which takes a finite number of steps, whereby one can determine either that the formula is a *theorem* or that it is not deducible. If the formula is a theorem, its interpretation

Consistency and the Decision-Problem

must give true propositions for all values of its variables; if the formula is not a theorem, it may be *self-consistent*, i.e. interpretable as true at least for some values of its variables, or else it is a *contradiction*. To establish that the formula is consistent is, of course, the same thing as showing that its contradictory is not a theorem. Now although one cannot tell off-hand whether the decision-problem is solvable, it is easy to anticipate the general conditions which a solution would have to satisfy. One condition is the existence of a property, let us call it the *K*-property, which only deducible formulas of the system have; the other condition is the possibility of establishing by a finite procedure with regard to any given formula whether it has the *K*-property. The solution of the decision-problem and of the problem of consistency does not yet mean that the postulational system is adequate as logic. Logic aims at a system of principles which are always true, i.e. it must consist of formulas which are true for all values of the variables. Hence the postulates for logic must enable one to sort without residue all the formulas within the system, i.e. all the formulas expressed in terms of the undefined elements of the system, into principles which are theorems and formulas whose claim to be always true is unfounded and which, therefore, are refutable. A system every formula of which is either deducible or refutable is called *complete*. The relation of completeness to consistency is this: completeness insures that at least one, consistency that at most one, of two contradictory formulas is a theorem.

The Problems of Logic

Confusion in a discussion of consistency might easily arise if the distinction between *postulational logic* and *postulational mathematics* is not brought out. A postulational system is a logic if it contains, besides variables, constant symbols which are interpretable as the propositional connectives "if-then" and "it is false that", or some equivalents of these, and the logical properties of which are defined by some of the postulates. A system is a mathematics if its constants are interpretable as mathematical operators or relations, such as "plus", "greater than", and the like, which do not connect propositions with one another. The presentation of the postulates for a mathematics requires either the medium of a symbolic logic or of an ordinary language. For example, the postulates for serial order can be given in terms of the undefined relation " $<$ ", by three statements in English:

(1) Given a class of elements K, if a and b are not the same elements of K, then either $a < b$ or $b < a$.

(2) Given a class of elements K, if $a < b$, then a and b are not the same elements of K.

(3) Given that a, b, c are elements of K, if $a < b$ and $b < c$, then $a < c$.

The same system can be formulated in the symbolism of the *Principia Mathematica*, if we let "fx" symbolize "x is an element of K" and "$g(x, y)$" stand for "$x < y$", as follows:

Consistency and the Decision-Problem

(1′) $[fa \cdot fb \cdot \sim(a = b)] \supset [g(a, b) \lor g(b, a)]$.

(2′) $[fa \cdot fb \cdot g(a, b)] \supset \sim(a = b)$.

(3′) $[fa \cdot fb \cdot fc \cdot g(a, b) \cdot g(b, c)] \supset g(a, c)$.

Although the primed system is entirely symbolic, and uses the propositional connectives "$\supset$" and "$\lor$", it is not logic, because its postulates do not define the properties of these connectives. The logic of implication and disjunction is presupposed throughout.

The distinction between a postulational logic and a postulational mathematics is relevant to the solution of the problem of consistency. In general, if consistency of the linguistic or symbolic medium of presentation is assumed, consistency of postulates for a mathematics is provable. The usual method of proof is by *interpretation*. If all postulates are satisfied by some concrete example, then in virtue of the principle that actuality cannot be inconsistent, the system which it exemplifies must also be consistent. For example, the system for serial order can be exemplified by the notes within an octave, if we interpret "$<$" as "lower (in pitch) than", since it is true that:

(1) If a and b are two different notes, then either a is lower than b or b is lower than a;
(2) If a is lower than b, they are different tones;
(3) If a is lower than b and b is lower than c, then a is lower than c.

And while the notes in their serial order of pitches

The Problems of Logic

are actually produced any time one runs his fingers over the keyboard of a piano, the consistency of the abstract conditions for serial order is thereby demonstrated. The weakness of the method of concrete interpretation is that there can be no assurance that concrete examples, such as the notes in their order of pitches, are available for any given set of mathematical postulates. But whenever they have no concrete examples on hand mathematicians can resort to *abstract interpretation*, and this means that consistency of a postulational mathematics is always provable.*

Of course, proof by interpretation is contingent

---

* Abstract interpretation gives a *schema* of an example instead of concrete examples such as the order of the notes in an octave and the like. Thus with regard to the system for serial order a *schema* may be constructed by taking three items such that while a serial relation holds between one item and each of the others, taken in that order and, between one and the other of the latter items, the same relation fails to hold for any other permutation of items. To give an illustration, while the serial relation of "being lower in pitch" holds between *do* and *re*, *do* and *mi*, and *re* and *mi*, it does not hold for *do* and *do*, *re* and *do*, *re* and *re*, *mi* and *do*, *mi* and *re*, and *mi* and *mi*. This concrete illustration, however, may be taken as an abstract schema provided we use *do*, *re*, *mi* not as the names of the notes C, D, E in the key of C, but as names of any given trio of items in abstraction from their nature. The consistency of the abstract example is seen if we observe that each singular statement as to whether the relation holds or not is concerned with a different permutation of the items and, therefore, all the singular statements which form the abstract example have a different subject-matter and so cannot be inconsistent. (For a more detailed exposition and its development, cf. Paul Henle, "A Definition of Abstract Systems," *Mind*, 1935.)

Consistency and the Decision-Problem

upon the assumption that the logic of the medium (within which the postulates for a mathematics are introduced) is itself consistent. Thus, from the postulationalist standpoint, the basic problem of consistency is concerned with a postulational logic rather than with mathematics. But here again a distinction has to be drawn. Logic may be *"pure"*, as exemplified by the calculus of unanalysed propositions and the calculus of predicate (cf. §§ 2 and 3), or combined with mathematics. The *"combined logic"* must list among its postulates some which determine the properties of certain constant symbols in a way which makes them interpretable as the basic mathematical relations of numerical equality and the like. In anticipation of the following sections it may be stated that the problems of consistency and completeness can be solved for a pure calculus, but not for a logic combined with mathematics. The proofs for "pure logic" are given in the order of increasing complexity of the systems concerned; first, for the calculus of unanalysed propositions; next, for the same calculus in combination with the logic of predicates.

§ 2. THE CALCULUS OF UNANALYSED PROPOSITIONS

Every symbolic postulational system is based upon a set of postulates which are expressed in terms of variables and undefined constant symbols. A set of postulates for the system of unanalysed propositions is given by the "primitive propositions" of section A of the *Principia*. In the modified version of *Grundzüge der theoretischen Logik* by Hilbert and Ackermann the set contains four formulas:

(a) $(p \lor p) \supset p$;
(b) $p \supset (p \lor q)$;
(c) $(p \lor q) \supset (q \lor p)$;
(d) $(p \supset q) \supset [(r \lor p) \supset (r \lor q)]$.

The primitive or undefined symbols are "$\sim$" (read "curl") and "$\lor$" (read "wedge"). The symbols "$\supset$", which appears in the formulation of the postulates, as well as the symbols "." and "$\equiv$" can always be omitted by means of the following definitions:

(1) "$p \supset q$" is defined as "$\sim p \lor q$"; (2) "$p \cdot q$" is defined as "$\sim (\sim p \lor \sim q)$"; and (3) "$p \equiv q$" is defined as "$(p \supset q) \cdot (q \supset p)$".

The theorems are derived from (a), (b), (c), (d) by (α) the rules of substitution and (β) the rule of inference.

(α) A given variable can be replaced at each of its occurrences within a formula by the same compound expression. For example, one can substitute "$q \lor r$" for "p" in (a) and derive the formula "$[(q \lor r) \lor (q \lor r)] \supset (q \lor r)$".

(β) From the conjunction of p and $p \supset q$ one can derive q.

This abstract system is called the calculus of unanalysed propositions because it is *interpretable* in terms of propositions taken as units, i.e. without regard to their constituents. Thus (b) can be inter-

Consistency and the Decision-Problem

preted as the assertion that "a proposition implies that either it or some other proposition is true".

The consistency of the calculus (taken in abstraction from its interpretations) can be proved by the test of the truth-table.* The test will convince one that (a), (b), (c), (d) are tautologies and that by means of (α) and (β) nothing but tautologies can be derived from tautologies. Hilbert and Ackermann give an analogous but simplified method of proof.

Let every variable be arbitrarily interpreted in one of two ways, as being either 0 or 1; let "∨" stand for the sign of arithmetical multiplication, and $\sim p$ be 1 if it stands for ~ 0, and 0 if it stands for ~ 1. With this interpretation every postulate gives 0. For example, taking (a) in the form "$\sim (p \vee p) \vee p$", one observes that at least one side of the main wedge must be interpreted as 0, and therefore the whole product is 0.† Furthermore, according to

---

* The use of the truth-table need not depend on logical intuition provided one does not interpret its symbols T and F (or 1 and 0) as, respectively, truth and falsehood. In abstraction from such an interpretation the truth-table is a table of permutations for two signs. The truth-function can then be defined by convention, i.e. by an arbitrary assignment of either T or F to each of their permutations. Thus we might assign T to the permutation $T\,T$ and F to all other permutations, and define this assignment as constitutive of a conjunction.

† For, by convention, p is either 1 or 0. Let p be 1. Then "$\sim (p \vee p) \vee p$" is "$\sim (1 \vee 1) \vee 1$", which is "$\sim 1 \vee 1$", i.e. "$0 \vee 1$", i.e. 0. Now let p be 0. Then the formula is "$\sim (0 \vee 0) \vee 0$". This gives "$\sim 0 \vee 0$", i.e. "$1 \vee 0$", i.e. 0. In either case (a) is 0.

The Problems of Logic

the rules (α) and (β) only *0* can be derived from the postulates each of which is *0*. Transformations by (α) cannot change either the range of arithmetical interpretation or the main structure of the original formulas, while, in applying (β), the premises p and $p \supset q$ can be identified with a pair of postulates only if each premise is *0*, and this is possible only when q is likewise *0*.* Since all theorems of the system must be interpreted as *0*, the system is *consistent*.† By a somewhat similar procedure the calculus is shown to be *complete*.

In order to solve the decision-problem one can begin by showing that every formula of the system is transformable into a standard pattern called the *conjunctive normal form*. The transformation is performed with the aid of the following rules (which are derivable from the postulates):

(a 1) The symbols "$\vee$" and "." have the associative, distributive and commutative properties;

(a 2) The symbols "$\sim(\sim p)$" and "p" can replace one another in any context;

(a 3) The symbol "$\sim(p \cdot q)$" is replaceable by the symbol "$\sim p \vee \sim q$", and the symbol "$\sim(p \vee q)$" by "$\sim p \cdot \sim q$";

---

* For if q were *1*, "$p \supset q$", i.e. "$\sim p \vee q$" would be "*1* $\vee$ *1*", i.e. *1*.

† If the system were inconsistent, both p and $\sim p$ would be theorems. But then at least one of them would be interpreted as *1*.

Consistency and the Decision-Problem

(b 1) $p \lor \sim p$ is a theorem;

(b 2) If p is a theorem and q is any formula, then $p \lor q$ is a theorem;

(b 3) If p is a theorem and q is a theorem, then $p \cdot q$ is a theorem.

Now let an expression be given for transformation into its normal form. By means of the definitions (1) and (3) it is cleared of the symbols "⊃" and "≡". By means of (a 3) the sign "∼" is made to precede only single variables. By means of (a 2) one gets rid of the reiterated "curl". Finally, by means of (a 1) the expression is formulated as a conjunction of disjunctions of *single proposition-variables with or without a single curl each*. This gives the normal conjunctive form. To illustrate each successive step of the transformation let the original expression be:

$$(p \supset q) \equiv (\sim q \supset \sim p).$$

The successive transformations are:

$(\sim p \lor q) \equiv (\sim\sim q \lor \sim p)$ (By def. (1)).

$(\sim p \lor q) \equiv (q \lor \sim p)$ (By (a 2)).

$[\sim(\sim p \lor q) \lor (q \lor \sim p)]$
  $\cdot [\sim(q \lor \sim p) \lor (\sim p \lor q)]$ (By def. (1) and (2)).

$[(\sim\sim p \cdot \sim q) \lor (q \lor \sim p)]$
  $\cdot [(\sim q \cdot \sim\sim p) \lor (\sim p \lor q)]$ (By (a 3)).

$[(p \cdot \sim q) \lor (q \lor \sim p)]$
  $\cdot [(\sim q \cdot p) \lor (\sim p \lor q)]$ (By (a 2)).

Applications of the distributive law give the conjunctive normal form:

$$(p \lor q \lor \sim p) \cdot (\sim q \lor q \lor \sim p) \\ \cdot (\sim q \lor \sim p \lor q) \cdot (p \lor \sim p \lor q).$$

The fact that every formula is reducible to its normal form leads to a solution of the decision problem because there exists a simple criterion which determines whether the given normal form is a theorem. It is a theorem when and only when in each member of the conjunction, i.e. in each set of disjunctions, at least one proposition-variable occurs once with and once without a curl. If this condition were not satisfied for some member of the conjunction, one could "force" this member to take the truth-value F (interpretable as "false") by assigning to each proposition-variable without a curl the value F and to each proposition-variable with a curl the value T (interpretable as "true"). And, of course, if at least one member of a conjunction is false, the whole conjunction is also false.

To give a simple example of a decision whereby the test by actual deduction is avoided let me take the formula:

$$p \supset (\sim p \supset q),$$

which is transformed into:

$$\sim p \lor p \lor q.$$

This is the normal form of the original expression, because it can be taken as a disjunction-member of a conjunction which has only one member. It is a theorem, because p occurs both with and without a curl. Observe that this theorem proves that any proposition can be deduced from an inconsistent set of postulates. For if a set is inconsistent, both p and $\sim p$ are deducible. But in conjunction with our theorem, p and $\sim p$ give q, which stands for any proposition.

§ 3. The Calculus of Pure Logic

The calculus of unanalysed propositions is a part of a system of pure logic which also contains formulas with constituents interpretable as *predicate-variables* (of the first order and type). If ϕ be such a constituent, the postulates of the system, in addition to (a), (b), (c), (d), of § 2, are:

(e) $[(x) \cdot \phi(x)] \supset \phi(y)$;
(f) $\phi(y) \supset [(\exists x) \cdot \phi(x)]$.

Besides these new postulates and an obvious extension of the rule of substitution to cover cases in which individual and predicate variables occur, the calculus of pure logic has two additional rules of inference:

(Υ 1) From "$p \supset \phi(x)$" one can derive
"$p \supset [(x) \cdot \phi(x)]$";
(Υ 2) From "$\phi(x) \supset p$" one can derive
"$[(\exists x) \cdot \phi(x)] \supset p$".

This form of a postulational system of logic can be interpreted as a logic of propositions with no

The Problems of Logic

bound-variables except individual-variables. Let us designate it by the initials P. L.

The proof of consistency of P. L. depends on the possibility of "reducing" its deducible formulas to the theorems of the calculus of unanalysed propositions. If such a "reduction"—to be called "p-reduction"—is possible for all deducible formulas of P. L., their contradictions cannot be p-reducible or else some of the theorems of the calculus of unanalysed propositions would have to be inconsistent with one another, which as already proved is not true. Hence if all deducible formulas of P. L. are p-reducible, P. L. must be a consistent system.

Now a formula of P. L., applied to a domain of k individuals (where "k" symbolizes some positive number), is called a "k-formula" if it is p-reducible. A p-reduction of a k-formula takes the following steps. First, the individual-variables of the original formula are replaced by values out of the domain of k individuals, $a_1, a_2, \ldots, a_k$; second, the prefixes of generality are eliminated by introducing instead conjunctions or disjunctions taken over the domain of k individuals; third, each of the propositional functions with arguments is replaced by a different proposition-variable.

To illustrate, let the original deducible formula be:

$$(x) \cdot [\phi\ x \supset ((\exists y) \cdot \phi y)].$$

Expansion by means of conjunction and disjunction gives:

$$[\phi\ a_1 \supset (\phi\ a_1 \vee \ldots \vee \phi\ a_k)] \ldots \ldots$$
$$[\phi\ a_k \supset (\phi\ a_1 \vee \ldots \vee \phi\ a_k)].$$

Consistency and the Decision-Problem

After the substitution of proposition-variables for the functions the formula becomes:

$$[p_1 \supset (p_1 \vee \ldots \vee p_k)] \ldots [p_k \supset (p_1 \vee \ldots \vee p_k)],$$

which is a theorem of the calculus of unanalysed propositions. This p-reduction shows that the original expression is a k-formula.

The consistency of P. L. can be proved because it is easy to prove that all its theorems are k-formulas. The theorems of the calculus of unanalysed propositions are seen to be k-formulas by immediate inspection. The postulate (e) is p-reducible to the theorem that a conjunction of proposition-variables implies one of them; and the postulate (f) is p-reducible to the theorem that a proposition-variable implies a disjunction of which it is a constituent. Thus both (e) and (f) are k-formulas. As to the rules $(\varUpsilon_1)$ and $(\varUpsilon_2)$, they are means of deriving k-formulas from k-formulas because they themselves correspond, respectively, to the theorems (of the propositional calculus) that "$p \supset (q_1 . q_2 \ldots q_k)$" is deducible from the premises "$p \supset q_1$", "$p \supset q_2$", ..., "$p \supset q_k$"; and that "$(q_1 \vee q_2 \vee \ldots \vee q_k) \supset p$" is deducible from the premises "$q_1 \supset p$", ..., "$q_k \supset p$".

While the problem of consistency is solved by proving that every theorem is a k-formula, the reverse, i.e. a proof that a k-formula is a theorem, would solve the decision-problem, since one can always test whether a given formula is a k-formula by the method of p-reduction. In conformity with this consideration the decision-problem has been solved for several kinds of formulas of P. L.

The Problems of Logic

First, k-formulas without bound variables are theorems because they can be derived by *substitution* [in accordance with the rules of *P. L.*] from the corresponding theorems of the calculus of unanalysed propositions.

Second, the decision-problem is solved for k-formulas with existential prefixes followed by expressions which contain k free variables. As an example, let the k-formula be:

$$(\exists z) . f(x, y, z).$$

In a domain of two individuals this formula gives:

$$f(x, y, x) \vee f(x, y, y),$$

which, as a 2-formula without bound variables, is a theorem. Let this theorem be a premise in conjunction with two others, which are established as special forms of postulate (f):

$$f(x, y, x) \supset [(\exists z) . f(x, y, z)];$$
$$f(x, y, y) \supset [(\exists z) . f(x, y, z)].$$

From these three premises the original k-formula is deducible and therefore it is a theorem.

Third, k-formulas of the second kind but preceded by non-existential prefixes for all its k variables are also theorems. This is so because the formulas:

$$(\exists y_1) \ldots (\exists y_r) . \phi(a, b, \ldots, k, y_1, \ldots, y_r);$$
$$(x_1) \ldots (x_k)(\exists y_1) \ldots (\exists y_r) . \phi(x_1, \ldots, x_k, y_1, \ldots, y_r),$$

can be proved to have equal deducibility; i.e. when one is a theorem so is the other.

Consistency and the Decision-Problem

Fourth, k-formulas of the so-called "unary calculus" whose constituent functions have each at most one argument are theorems because they can be reduced to formulas of the third kind. This kind of reduction is a transformation of the original expression into its "prenex" normal form, i.e. a form in which all prefixes precede a matrix which is derived by substitution from the corresponding conjunctive normal form of the calculus of unanalysed propositions.

There is no need to proceed into further details for a general account of the decision-problem. In principle the problem remains unsolved, because there are k-formulas which are not theorems of $P.\ L.$: these are contradictories of formulas which can be satisfied only in an infinite domain of individuals. Consider the formula:

$$(F)\ (x)\ .\ \sim \phi\ (x, x)\ .\ \Big\{[(x, y, z) : \phi\ (x, y)\ .\ \phi\ (y, z)] \supset \phi\ (x, z)\Big\}\ .\ (x)\ (\exists\ y)\ .\ \phi\ (x, y).$$

Its interpretations will show that it cannot be satisfied by any finite number of individuals. For example, if "$\phi\ (x, y)$" is interpreted as "the integer x is smaller than the integer y", then it is not true, except for an infinite number of integers, that "$(x)\ (\exists\ y)\ .\ \phi\ (x, y)$" holds, i.e. that for every integer x there exists a greater integer y. Since the formula (F) cannot be true in any finite domain of individuals, its *contradictory* must be true for all finite domains of individuals and so must be a k-formula. Nevertheless this *k*-formula is not a theorem, since it fails when *k* is an infinite number.

§ 4. Gödel's Contribution

When logic is combined with mathematics, either in the logistic manner of the *Principia* (where mathematical notions and statements are resolved into purely logical constituents) or by the addition of mathematical axioms to the postulates of the pure calculus, it can be shown that the combined system contains "undecidable" propositions, is incomplete, and that its consistency is not provable. These are the "negative" results of Gödel's work. At the same time, and in the course of his argument, Gödel has established that the unqualified "vicious-circle" principle is wrong and that propositions within a sufficiently rich language can be about themselves unless they qualify themselves as true, false, or in some other epistemological way.

Gödel's procedure can be divided into three main stages, to be designated as stage I, II, and III. In I a formal system, comprehensive enough to be interpreted as a combined logic and arithmetic, is introduced. This formal object-system will be referred to by the initials $F.\ S.$ In II the system $F.\ S.$ is conventionally represented, we shall say "*arithmetized*", by another system in terms of positive integers. In III special expressions of $F.\ S.$ are constructed with the aid of the arithmetized representations, and these expressions are then interpretable as describing themselves. Some of them are found to be undecidable formulas. We now shall go over these three divisions at a greater length.

I

The formal object-system $F.\ S.$ can be built up by adding to the pure calculus of logic of § 3 a few primitive elements and postulates which have an arithmetical interpretation. The additional primitive elements (or undefined terms) are:

(1) O (to be interpreted as "the number of zero").

(2) N (to be interpreted as "the successor of" a given number).

(3) $\mathcal{E}$ (to be used as a prefix in expressions of the form "$(\mathcal{E}\,x)\,.\,\phi\,x$" which stands for "the smallest integer x such that $\phi\,x$, if there exists an x such that $\phi\,x$; otherwise . . . zero").

For convenience of abbreviation the numbers O, $N(O)$, $N(N(O))$, etc., will be written as z_0, z_1, z_2, etc. Thus z_6 is an abbreviation for "six". The abbreviations in terms of the z's will be called "*transcriptions*". In describing $F.\ S.$ we shall make use of another abbreviation. Instead of writing "the expression obtained from ϕ by substituting the letter a for each occurrence of the free variable x within ϕ" we shall write "Subst $(\phi\,{}^x_a)$".

The postulates of $F.\ S.$ (in addition to the postulates (a), (b), (c), (d), (e), (f) of § 3) are:

The Problems of Logic

(g) $x = x$.

(h) $x = y \mathrel{.} \equiv \mathrel{.} \phi(x) = \phi(y)$.

(k) $(x = y) \mathrel{.} (y = z) \mathrel{.} \supset \mathrel{.} x = y$.

(l) $\sim (O = N(x))$.

(m) $N(x) = N(y) \mathrel{.} \supset \mathrel{.} x = y$.

(n) The Principle of Mathematical Induction: From $\phi(o)$ and $\phi(y) \supset \phi N(y)$, $\phi(y)$ can be deduced.

The postulates (g), (h), and (k) determine the properties of the sign "$=$" to be interpreted as numerical equality: a number is equal to itself; when x is equal to y, one can replace the other in any context ϕ, and *vice versa*; equality is a transitive relation.

The interpretation of (l) is that zero has no predecessor: the system $F. S.$ is concerned with positive integers. According to (m) no two numbers have the same successor.

In addition to the rules of procedure of the pure calculus the system $F. S.$ contains rules of operation with the prefix $\mathcal{E}$ which are entirely analogous, *mutatis mutandis*, to the rules which regulate the use of the existential and non-existential prefixes.

This sums up the formal properties of $F. S.$

II

The primitive elements of $F. S.$ are discrete entities, they are countable. And any written expression of $F. S.$ must obviously be a finite sequence of primitive elements. Hence it is possible to assign arbitrarily, as a label, a different positive integer to every different expression (whether it is a primitive element or a combination of such) in $F. S.$ This labelling of symbols in $F. S.$ is the first step of *arithmetization*.

To arithmetize the *primitive elements* we write under each of them its representing number:

0	N	$=$	$\sim$	$\vee$	.	$\supset$	$\equiv$	$\exists$	ε	(	)
1	2	3	4	5	6	7	8	9	10	11	12

Any integer > 13 and $\equiv 0 \pmod{3}$, i.e. any integer which being divided by 3 gives no residue, such as 15, 18, etc., will be employed to label *proposition-variables* p, q, etc.

An integer > 13 and $\equiv 1 \pmod{3}$, such as 16, 19, etc., will represent *number-variables*, x, y, etc.

An integer > 13 and $\equiv 2 \pmod{3}$, such as 17, 20, etc., will label a function-variable, ϕ, ψ, etc.

Obviously a *formula*, as a sequence of primitive elements, can be arithmetized by a sequence of the numbers representing these elements. But it is desirable to label each formula by a single number. Let the original arithmetization of a formula be a certain sequence of positive integers:

$$k, k, \ldots, k.$$

It can be correlated with a *single number* defined as the product:

$$2^{k_1} \cdot 3^{k_2} \cdot \ldots \cdot p_n^{k_n},$$

The Problems of Logic

where p_n is the nth prime number in their order of magnitude.

For example, take the formula in *F. S.*:

$$x = 0$$

As a sequence it is arithmetized into:

16, 3, 1.

To give it a single number as a label, we must compute the product:

$$2^{16} \cdot 3^3 \cdot 5^1 = 65536 \cdot 27 \cdot 5.$$

Proofs are sequences of formulas, of which the last is the conclusion. Accordingly a proof is arithmetized by substituting for each of the constituent-formulas its representative single number. The resulting sequence of numbers can be correlated in its turn with a unique positive integer.

The arithmetization of symbols, formulas, and proofs gives a *one-one correspondence*. Each element or combination of elements in *F. S.* is represented by a different number. Conversely, given the representing integer of a formula, the latter can be "retrieved", because the factorization of a product into its prime factors, which represent the elements of the formula, is unique.

The class of representing positive integers can now be organized into a *system*. The purpose of this organization is to represent within the arithmetized medium *theoretical* (or, according to the postulationalists, metalogical) considerations about the object-system *F. S.*, such as the statement that "a certain formula of *F. S.* is deducible from another formula of *F. S.*" Thus the arithmetized system consists of *functions* and *relations* of positive integers which can be explained by reference to the theoretical (or metalogical) functions and relations of formulas of *F. S.* As an illustrative selection a few symbols of the arithmetized system are given in the left-hand side column; their elucidation in terms of the theory of the system *F. S.* is given on the right-hand side.

Each of these symbols of arithmetization can be defined directly, i.e. without reference to *F. S.* The direct definitions given in Gödel's original article, although cumbersome technically, have the advantage of showing that all the functions and relations of the arithmetized system are *recursive*.*

---

* "$\phi(x_1, \ldots, x_n)$ shall be said to be *recursive* with respect to $\psi(x_1, \ldots, x_{n-1})$ and $\chi(x_1, \ldots, x_{n+1})$ if, for all natural numbers

$\phi(0, x_2, \ldots, x_n) = \psi(x_2, \ldots, x_n)$;
$\phi(k + 1, x_2, \ldots, x_n) = \chi(k, \phi(k, x_2, \ldots, x_n), x_2, \ldots, x_n)$."

(K. Gödel, *On Undecidable Propositions*, 1934, Princeton.)

The pair of equations gives a recursive definition of the function. In special cases of recursive definition any variables on the right side of the equations can be omitted in any of its occurrences; in the simplest case the right side of the first equation is a number as in:

$$f(1) = 1;$$
$$f(n + 1) = f(n) \cdot (n + 1),$$

which gives a recursive definition of the function:

$$f(n) = 1 \cdot 2 \ldots n$$

A recursive function is computable, i.e. replaceable by a number, in a finite number of steps, because it must be either a function of *1* or of some other number $(n + 1)$. If it is a function of *1*, the first equation of its definition immediately gives its numerical value. If

[*Continued on page* 111

The Problems of Logic

$Neg(x)$	The number which arithmetizes $\sim p$, if x arithmetizes p, where p and $\sim p$ are formulas of $F.S.$; otherwise it is zero.
$Sb\left(x_{N_y}^{a}\right)$	The arithmetization of Subst $\left(\phi_{z_y}^{w}\right)$, if x, N_y, and a are, respectively, arithmetizations of ϕ, z_y, w.
$Sb(x, y)$ (An abbreviation of the preceding symbol)	
$n\,G\,L\,x$	The nth member of the sequence of positive integers correlated with the product x. Let the sequence be: $k_1, k_2, \ldots, k_k, \ldots, k_n, \ldots, k_r$. Then: $x = 2^{k_1} \ldots p_m^{k_n} \ldots p_q^{k_r}$; and $n\,G\,L\,x = k_n$.
$L(x)$	The number of members in the sequence arithmetized by x.
$P(x)$	x arithmetizes a proof in $F.\,S.$
$x\,P\,y$	x arithmetizes a proof of a formula which is arithmetized by y.
Consist.	$F.\,S.$ is a consistent system.

Consistency and the Decision-Problem

III

At this stage of the argument we shall use "transcriptions" of the expressions of $F. S.$ in terms of the z's with subscripts. Let $\phi(m, n, \ldots) = k$, where $m, n, \ldots$, and k are positive integers.

Then $\phi(m, n, \ldots)$ is transcribed into $g(z_m, z_n, \ldots)$ provided $g(z_m, z_n, \ldots) = z_k$. A relation

Continued from page 109]

it is $\phi(n+1)$, where $n \neq 0$, it is computable as the function ψ of two arguments which, eventually, are shown to be numbers. For n stands for a number, while $\phi(n)$ is either the number a, if $n = 1$, or it is the function ψ of two arguments, n and $\phi(n-1)$. The regression in computation is from $\phi(n+1)$, through $\phi(n)$, to $\phi(n-1)$, and so on until the argument of ϕ is reduced to 1, which is bound to happen no matter how large n is.

Let "summation" be the function to be written as "sum $(k, x_2, \ldots, x_n)$."

The recursive definition of "summation" is given, for two numbers, by the equations:

sum $(O, y) = y$;
sum $(N(x), y) = N(\text{sum}(x, y))$, where N stands for "successor".

Let x and y be, respectively, 2 and 1. Then the repeated application of the second equation gives:

$$\begin{aligned}\text{sum}(3, 1) &= N(\text{sum}(2, 1)) \\ &= N(N(\text{sum}(1, 1))) \\ &= N(N(N(\text{sum}(0, 1)))).\end{aligned}$$

By means of the first equation of the recursive definition the last expression is transformed into "$N(N(N(1)))$" which gives 4 as the value of "sum $(3, 1)$".

A *relation* R of positive integers $x_1, \ldots, x_n$, to be written as "$R(x_1, \ldots, x_n)$" is recursive if its "associated" function ϕ is recursive. A function ϕ is "associated" with the relation R when the following conditions are satisfied: $\phi(x_1, \ldots, x_n) = 0$, if the relation R holds for the same numbers, and $\phi(x_1, \ldots, x_n) = 1$, if R does not hold, i.e. if $\sim R$.

The Problems of Logic

$R(m, n, \ldots)$ is transcribed by means of transcribing its "associated" function.*

Now Gödel has proved (and the reader is referred for the proof to Gödel's original paper) that all *recursive* functions and relations of positive integers can be transcribed in terms of z's. But the symbols of the arithmetized system stand for recursive functions and relations of the representing integers. Hence they can also be transcribed, which means that they can be formulated within $F. S.$ And since all of them (in their theoretical explanation or import) refer to $F. S.$, in transcription they become expressions of $F. S.$ which are about expressions of $F. S.$ In special cases some of them are statements about themselves, just as the syntactical statement that "Every English sentence contains a verb" happens to be in English, and therefore is about itself.

Consider the formula $U(w)$ of $F. S.$ in the construction of which two other formulas of $F. S.$ are employed: $D(u, v)$ which is the transcription of the arithmetized relation $x \, P \, y$; and $S(u, v)$ which is the transcription of the symbol $S \, b \, (x, y)$. The definition of $U(w)$ is given below on the first line of the right-hand side column; its representing number or arithmetization is given on the same line on the left-hand side.

---

p	$U(w) = (v) . \sim D(v, S(w, w))$. Def.
$S \, b \, (p, p)$	$U(z_p)$

* For the definition of an "associated" function see the last paragraph of the preceding footnote.

Consistency and the Decision-Problem

Thus p is the representing number of $U(w)$. If we substitute z_p for w in $U(w)$, the result is symbolized by "Subst $\left(U(w)_{z_p}^{w}\right)$", and the representing number of this symbol is $S\,b\,(p, p)$. The expansion of $U(z_p)$, in accordance with the definition of $U(w)$, gives:

(1). $U(z_p) = (v) \,.\, \sim D\,(v, S\,(z_p, z_p))$.

We can now show that $U(z_p)$ is interpretable as a formula which is about itself. First, let the definitions of $U(w)$ be abbreviated as $F(S(w, w))$ and let one of the arbitrary interpretations of $F(z_n)$ be that "the number which is transcribed as z_n, i.e. the number n, arithmetizes a formula which has the property f". Next, we determine the number which is transcribed by $S(z_p, z_p)$; it is "the number of the formula which results from the formula whose number is p when z_p is substituted for its free variable", i.e. it is "$S\,b\,(p, p)$". This number represents a formula which has, so we learn from our interpretation of $F(S(z_p, z_p))$, the property f. But since this number is the number of $F(S(z_p, z_p))$, i.e. of $U(z_p)$, the latter ascribes to itself the property f.* Thus $U(z_p)$ is an expression which is about itself. This invalidates Russell's "vicious-circle" principle. At the same time it gives an instance of an *undecidable* proposition, i.e. it can be neither proved nor disproved.

Suppose $U(z_p)$ is provable. Then there exists (in

* If we let f stand for "false", then $F(S(z\,p, z\,p))$ becomes a formulation of "This proposition is false", which is intended to apply to itself.

The Problems of Logic

the arithmetized system) a number k such that $k\,P\,S\,b\,(p, p)$. In transcription this gives:

(2) $D\,(z_k,\,S\,(z_p,\,z_p)\,)$.

On the other hand it follows from (1) that, for the value k of v:

(3) $\sim D\,(z_k,\,S\,(z_p,\,z_p)\,)$.

But (2) and (3) contradict one another. Hence if $F.\,S.$ is a consistent system, $U(z_p)$ is not provable.

Suppose $U(z_p)$ is refutable, i.e. $\sim U(z_p)$ is provable. This would mean that $\sim (v)\,.\,(\sim D\,(v,\,S\,(z_p,\,z_p)\,)$, i.e. there exists a number k for which $D\,(z_k,\,S\,(z_p,\,z_p)\,)$ holds. On the other hand, since $U(z_p)$ is not provable, $\sim D\,(z_k,\,S\,(z_p,\,z_p)\,)$ should hold for all k. Thus the supposition that $U(z_p)$ is refutable also leads to inconsistency.

The fact that $U(z_p)$ is undecidable can be used to show that there is no proof of the consistency of the system $F.\,S.$ For if $F.\,S.$ is consistent, $U(z_p)$ is not provable. In the arithmetized system this gives:

$$\text{Consist}\,.\,\supset\,[(x)\,.\,\sim (x\,P\,S\,b\,(p, p)\,)]$$

The transcription of this implication is provable. And if the transcribed "consist" were provable $U(z_p)$, the transcribed consequent would be provable, and this, we know, is not the case unless $F.\,S.$ is inconsistent.

Thus neither the problems of consistency and completeness, nor the decision-problem, can be solved for logic which is combined with arithmetic.

Consistency and the Decision-Problem

These so-called negative results have forced the postulationalists to admit that a formal logic cannot be a comprehensive system, that a common language such as English is comprehensive at the price of being inconsistent, and that there is an unending hierarchy of consistent languages arranged in the order of increasing comprehensiveness.

To an intuitionalist Gödel's results are negative in a different sense. They show that postulational systems are always inadequate as expressions of the logic of intuition. Whether this is so because formulations in terms of clear-cut symbols are too stiff to do full justice to involved ramifications and flexible turns of logical thought, is a matter for general speculation. To be more specific, one might argue against mixing up formulas of logic and mathematics. For so long as logic is kept clear of infinite domains, the decision-problem together with the problems of consistency and completeness are solved. And if trouble begins with the infinite, it is bound to come when arithmetic of positive integers, which are infinite in number, is joined with logic. On the other hand, one might look for a deeper source of evil. One might, for example, suspect that the undecidable formula $U(z_p)$ is "about itself" in a sense which needs further analysis. This formula has a certain representing number, and when interpreted, it refers to itself as to "the formula which has that number"; but this reference is a definite description, and the question of how the reference by description is possible is far from being explored. Let $U(z_p)$ be irreproachable within the abstract framework of a postulational system or even as a mathematical formula, in a larger context of interpretation its "reference to itself" may be a confusion between proposition and propositional function, as indeed one of the interpretations of $U(z_p)$, "This proposition is false", was shown to be.

Chapter IV

CONCEPTUAL REFERENCE

§ 1. Introduction

Objective reference is an element of significance and not of meaning. This is so because of the fact that while the connotative content changes from one proposition to another, all of them are invariably about something. This something is objective in the sense that a proposition which is about it, unless purely verbal, does not refer to a mere word or even to the connotation of the word but to a thing. For example, when I say that I am fond of tennis, I do not mean that I am fond of the word "tennis" or of its definition, I am concerned with the game itself as an actual exercise and enjoyment. It would seem that in speaking or writing about things, one is in contact with extra-linguistic actuality. Hence arises the Paradox of objective reference: "There exists *within* discourse an objective for reference the nature of which is to be something *outside* discourse."

This Paradox is not avoided by treating language as the result of conventions of formation and transformation of sentences. However conventional the basis of a language may be, it must allow, to use Carnap's terminology, for the distinction between real object-sentences and pseudo-object-sentences. Let us illustrate this distinction by Carnap's own examples: he contrasts "Babylon was a big town" as

The Problems of Logic

an object-sentence with "Babylon was treated of in yesterday's lecture" as a pseudo-object-sentence.* Suppose, for the sake of argument, that Carnap is right when he asserts that the second sentence is verbal, i.e. is about the word "Babylon", because it can be translated without loss of meaning into "the word 'Babylon' occurred in yesterday's lecture". This does not explain why the first sentence is not verbal, i.e. how it can be about the town itself. Both sentences use the same word "Babylon", and I think both use it as a definite description, i.e. as an equivalent for the phrase "the ancient city in the Euphrates valley", and not as a name.† Certainly Babylon cannot be used now as a name except by a traveller in Iraq and even then only as a name of certain ruins and not of a once prosperous city. But if "Babylon" is used as a description, it certainly does not *refer to* a phrase or descriptive conception such as the phrase or conception of "the ancient

---

* Op. cit., p. 286.

† The reader may wish to be reminded of Russell's distinction between names and descriptions. The sole meaning of a name is its denotation, therefore in the absence of the denoted object a name becomes a meaningless utterance. If I say "Ed. Hampton", the hearer does not get any meaning unless the person thus named has been introduced to him. The meaning of a name is the actual presentation of which it is simply a label. A description, on the other hand, is meaningful regardless of whether it denotes anything at all. Thus "the ghost of Kentersville" is a phrase which one can understand just as well as the description "der Führer". Sometimes a word which up to a certain date had been used as a name is later turned into a symbol for a description. For example, after 1825 the word "Napoleon" has been used as an abbreviation for "the first Emperor of France".

Conceptual Reference

city in the Euphrates Valley". For when one says that "Babylon was a big town" one does not utter the nonsense that "the phrase (or conception of) the ancient city in the Euphrates Valley is a big town". The phrase or conception is only a means for a reference to something which is, presumably, beyond discourse. Of course, Carnap does not deny the existence of such an objective reference. The point is that conceptional reference must be recognized even by the postulationalists. But they fail to explain how it is possible, because their identification of discourse with conventionally regulated languages must assume reference, which is extra-linguistic and therefore beyond convention, to be a complete mystery.

The postulationalist might retort that the difficulty, which I am concerned with, is a matter of the epistemology of contingent statements of fact, with no bearing upon logic as a formal calculus developed in abstraction from interpretation. In order to bring such an abstract logic in contact with actuality, there is no need for conceptual reference since interpretation can be performed without the aid of discourse by a direct correlation between the postulational system and the ontological structure. For example, if the symbols, x, y, etc., of the postulational set for serial order are assigned as labels of boxes to a Chinese nest of boxes, the function g, which relates the symbols to one another, is perceptually exemplified as an insertion of the smaller boxes within their larger containers. Whether such examples establish the postulationalist point that interpretation as an observable concrete illustration of an abstract system dispenses with conceptual reference altogether is questionable. But even if one should answer the question in the negative, the postulationalists would still be right in disregarding conceptual reference so far as logic is confined to computations of deduction within the abstract system or, to put it more simply, so far as one "plays logic" as a game. This is of course true, yet the game of logic is not the whole of logic. The postulationalists themselves are forced to recognize besides the object-logic its metalogic, and there, along with metalogical references to the formulas of the object-system, the Paradox of conceptual reference makes its entry. As an example, let the formula of the object-logic be:

(1) $\qquad p \supset q.$

Metalogically this formula is referred to by means of inverted commas: "$p \supset q$". But this device, i.e. the reference of "$p \supset q$" to formula (1), can be used neither in metalogic, which puts the object-formulas in quotation marks, nor in logic, where they are always free from quotation marks. In order to make a statement of reference in which the same formula can be used both with and without quotation marks, a neutral medium of language, different from either logic or metalogic, would seem to be indispensable. Tarski has worked out such a medium in his *semantics*, which he defines as

". . . the whole of speculations that concern themselves with those concepts in which, roughly speaking, are expressed certain correlations between the

Conceptual Reference

expressions of a language and the objects and facts indicated by them."*

One of Tarski's examples of a semantic statement is the proposition:

The expression "the conqueror of Iena" symbolizes Napoleon Bonaparte.

If "Napoleon Bonaparte" were short for a descriptive phrase, the proposition would be a correlation of two linguistic expressions. And if semantics could be confined exclusively to correlations of linguistic forms, it would give a medium between metalogic and logic without raising the problem of transcendent reference. But if Tarski were dealing with *linguistic* correlations he should have thought of a less ambiguous proposition, for example, of the proposition:

The expression "the conqueror of Iena" symbolizes the prisoner of St. Helena.

Moreover, his definition of semantics makes it practically certain that he intended to establish a medium of reference from linguistic expressions to the corresponding extra-linguistic objects. The fact is that semantics cannot be confined to purely linguistic relationships because it contains such concepts as "truth", which in the sense of "agreement with reality" involves a reference beyond discourse. This sense is not repudiated, but only made more precise, in the contextual definition of truth which Tarski himself gives:

". . . we will recognize as correct all such sentences as: *the proposition 'it is snowing' is true if and only if*

* A. Tarski, "Grundlegung der wissenshaftlichen Semantic", *Actes du congrès international de philosophie scientifique*," Paris, 1936.

The Problems of Logic

it is snowing; the proposition 'the world war will begin in 1936' *is true if and only if the world war will begin in* 1936; in general every sentence of the form: *the proposition x is true if and only if p*, where '*p*' is to be replaced by any proposition of the language investigated and '*x*' by any proper name of the proposition, whereby the proper name belongs to the province of the metalanguage".

This passage discloses as clearly as one can wish the failure of semantics to do justice to the notion of "agreement with reality" with its implication of objective reference. The intended reference is from discourse to actuality; what semantics offers instead is a reference from metalogical expression to an expression of the object-language. The original intention cannot be realized by the simple device of putting the metalogical statements in inverted commas. The whole correlation remains within discourse, and the paradox of transcendent reference is not resolved. Furthermore, the identification of discourse with language (or with postulational systems) leaves no hope for a possible resolution of the Paradox, because the discontinuity between language and extra-linguistic actuality is obvious and final.

If the postulationalist efforts to deal with objective reference are instructive, the instruction is that of a negative example: it suggests a remedy for their shortcomings. This is a rejection of the assumption that language and discourse are co-extensive. Instead I shall assume that discourse involves, besides mere words, concepts, and in order to solve the Paradox of reference I shall argue that conceptual discourse

Conceptual Reference

is not discontinuous with extra-linguistic actuality. There is no paradox of self-transcendence, if discourse can be in contact with actuality, for then one might reach the latter without leaving the grounds of the former. My theory is that where discourse goes beyond language, elements are found which belong at once to conception and to external reality. Let me specify this theory within the framework of the doctrine of logical significance. The elements within a proposition can be divided into two kinds according to their *mode* of significance: there are *descriptive* elements whose significance is to refer to other elements by way of description, and there are elements which present *objectives for reference*, i.e. which are referred to or described without describing or referring to anything themselves. Predicates and relations are elements of the descriptive kind; they form pure discourse, which as contrasted with actuality is co-extensive with what Carnap would call language together with its syntax. Objectives for reference, on the other hand, go beyond pure discourse, because, as an examination of *perceptual judgments* will show, they are elements which are common to the fields of conception and actuality.

A perceptual judgment involves as a constituent a proper name or a demonstrative symbol, such as "this", and is thereby a statement directly about a *presentation*. Thus when I make the judgment that "this is white", unless I explain to you that I mean this page of the book you are reading and thereby make you face the same presentation that I have, my judgment would not be fully understood. A

The Problems of Logic

presentation is, therefore, what the judgment of perception is about, and since a presentation is a manifestation of actuality, the point that the objective for reference can belong to both discourse and actuality is made. It would be false to think that as a constituent of a judgment a presentation ceases to be a manifestation of actuality, for the presentation would be there, where it is apprehended, exactly the same even if the judgment were never passed upon it. On the other hand, it is true that the presentation plays its part of an objective for reference only through the framework of a judgment. Hence the capacity of being an objective is a mode of significance derived from discourse.* Presentations may

---

* Consider a bare presentation, for example, the presentation of Fig. 1.

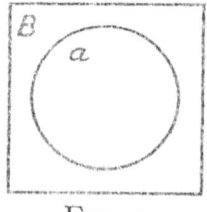

Fig. 1

This presentation is different from the perceptual judgment that "a is inside b". My cat looking at Fig. 1 would have the same, or at least a similar, presentation to mine without being able to make the corresponding judgment. The difference is that the judgment requires a conceptual analysis and comparison of elements which in the bare presentation are fused into a complex but unified *gestalt*. Thus the judgment "a is inside b" is not about the bare presentations a and b, since as such they are not given in separation from one another, but is to be understood, rather in the sense that "The

Conceptual Reference

change, succeeding one another, and yet each can in turn fulfil the office of an objective for reference in discourse. Hence, even without an exhibition of the corresponding presentation, the statement "this is white" is more than the incomplete form ". . . is white"; although the former is not a judgment of perception, unless its objective for reference enframes a presentation, the statement is about something, it has an objective for reference, and can be interpreted by the reader as the proposition that "the circle a is inside the square b", or "The figure a is inside the figure b", where a and b have been distinguished from one another by means of the enframing concepts "circle", "square", or "figure". Accordingly the objectives for reference, i.e. the things that the judgment is about, are *conceptualized presentations*. While such conceptualized presentations demonstrate continuity between discourse and existence, they also suggest that even when the presentations are removed from these conceptual frames, the latter may continue to serve as objectives for reference, as exemplified in the replacement of the perceptual judgment "a is inside b" by the purely conceptual proposition "The circle is inside the square".

One might object to my identification of the perceptual judgment "a is inside b" with its conceptualized form "The figure a is inside the figure b" on the ground that the latter itself presupposes perceptual judgments, such as "a is a figure", which still are about bare presentations a or b. My answer is in a further identification of "a is a figure" with "The thing a is a figure". It brings out the point that an objective for reference must be more transparent, not as rich in connotation, than either "circle" or "figure". Sometimes "thing" is said to be too generic and poor in content to be a genuine concept. With this I should agree if concepts were always means of describing or of referring to something; but the existence of concepts as objects to be referred to, i.e. as frameworks of presentations, makes it clear that the more inobtrusive such concepts the better they are.

The Problems of Logic

thing which the author is concerned with is white". While the fact that an objective for reference may coincide with a presentation in a conceptual framework gives a resolution to the Paradox of transcendent reference, the possibility of objectives to exist independently of presentations as mere conceptual frameworks is relevant to the problem of reference in *pure discourse*, in which there are no judgments of perception but only communicable propositions given entirely in terms of concepts.

§ 2. EXISTENTIAL PROPOSITIONS

An explanation of conceptual reference in discourse is primarily concerned with general existential propositions because any other non-compound proposition can be analysed as a combination of existential propositions with their negations.* Existential

---

* The so-called universal or non-existential propositions are negations of existential propositions. For example, "No men are mortal" means that *it is false that there exist mortal men*. The singular propositions which involve definite descriptions, i.e. phrases of the form "the so-and-so", are analysed, following Russell, into a compound (conjunction) of existential and non-existential propositions. To quote from Russell:

Thus the proposition "the author of *Waverley* was Scotch", for example, involves:

(1) "x wrote *Waverley*" is not always false;
(2) "if x and y wrote *Waverley*, x and y are identical" is always true;
(3) "if x wrote *Waverley*, x was Scotch" is always true.

... Hence the three together may be taken as defining what is meant by the proposition "the author of *Waverley* was Scotch".—(*Introduction to Mathematical Philosophy*, p. 177, Allen & Unwin.) In this conjunction, (1) is an existential, and (2) and (3) are non-existential forms.

Conceptual Reference

propositions are expressed by sentences in which, at least grammatically, predication of "existence" takes place. The qualification "at least grammatically" is made because there is a kind of existential statement which is very trivial but which contains "existence" as a genuine constituent and not merely as a grammatical predicate. "This page exists", "propositions exist", "Illusion exists", are typical examples. The "trivial" existential statements register the presence of a thing (which might be a presentation or a mathematical entity or anything whatsoever) within its own medium, and do not contain a reference from one medium to another, in particular from thought to actuality. Perhaps the least trivial predication of "existence" in statements of this kind is an assertion of conceivability, i.e. an assertion about something that it is present in the medium of conception, as when a mathematician says that complex numbers exist without intending to assert that they are real outside the domain of mathematics but merely meaning that within a consistent mathematical system they have specifiable relationships to other mathematical entities. In this, as in other cases of trivial statements of existence, the entertainment of an entity by means of a statement is equivalent to the entity's realization. Thus even false propositions exist in the trivial sense, because they are entertained in thought, which means that as propositions they are realizable although they cannot be realized among facts. It follows that the understanding of a trivial existential proposition proves it to be true, since in order to understand one must have at least the *conceptual construction* and, therefore, the existence of the entity of which "existence" is predicated. Of course, instead of conceptual constructions an actual presentation can be the subject of existential predication, but the presence of a presentation is such an obvious truism that, disregarding it, one can deny the existence of certain presentations, using "existence" in another, non-trivial sense, to be explained presently, without serious danger of ambiguity. Thus one denies the existence of dreams, although one knows very well that as dreams they appear and therefore exist. Objective reference raises no problem so far as the trivial existential statements are concerned: their object for reference is always present as a constituent, since the very purpose of the predication of "existence" is to register this presence.

The non-trivial existential proposition is a perfect instance of conceptual reference, for it asserts that a certain concept has realization outside the language or discourse. But no constituent of such a proposition corresponds to the grammatical predicate of "existence" in its verbal expression. For example, take the sentence "Man exists". If the verb "exists" stood for one of the constituents of the proposition, then another of its constituents would have to correspond to the word "man". But it is obvious that no genuine particular entity can be denoted as the exemplification of "man". Every real man is a Mr. Brown or a Mr. Jones or some other individual and it is incredible that there should be a single concrete being who is a man in general but no one in particular. Hence, as Russell has explained it, the propo-

Conceptual Reference

sition expressed by the sentence "Man exists" is not about "man", but about the corresponding adjectival description "human" to the effect that this description is not a mere conception but has realization. Now to say that the adjective "human" has realization is the same as saying that at least one proposition of the kind to which "Whitehead is human", "The lizard is human", and the like belong, is true. Accordingly, "Man exists" means that a true proposition, in which the predication of the adjective "human" takes place, can be found. In this interpretation "Man exists" is seen to be neither about a "man" nor about "existence" but about the truth-value of a certain proposition which involves the predication of "human". If we let f stand for "human", we can give to "Man exists" the symbolic form:

$$(\exists x) . f(x)$$

which is read "there exists an x such that x has the property f". This is equivalent to saying that "there exists a true value (a proposition) of the function $f(x)$".

One might think that this analysis must lead to an infinite regress. One begins with "Man exists" only to replace it by expressions of the same form "there exists an x . . ." or "there exists a true proposition . . ." which therefore must be in their turn analysed, and so on. In fact this would be a correct criticism, if Russell were right in his belief that the non-trivial use of "existence" is the only one that makes sense. Contrary to his opinion I have argued that there are trivial existential propositions, and it seems to me that the readings "there exists an x . . ." and "there exists a true proposition . . ." are instances of the predication of existence in a trivial sense, because if they were not, they would involve an infinite regress, e.g. "there exists an x . . ." would mean "there exists a y such that it is x-like . . .", and so on. Thus, if my view is correct, any non-trivial existential proposition involves a trivial one, while the reverse, of course, does not hold.

This point is a virtual explanation of conceptual reference. The condition which an objective for reference must satisfy is its capacity of being described without giving a description; as we already found this condition is fulfilled by the subject of a trivial existential statement. Now we learn that a non-trivial existential proposition must contain as a component a trivial existential statement, and we can conclude that the subject of the latter is the objective for reference of the former. We need only remind ourselves that since the conception of the subject of a trivial statement is identical with its realization, we observe here a contact between thought and reality which was required for discourse concerned with things rather than with words or ideas. An entity where conception and reality meet and which, therefore, serves as an objective for reference in discourse, will be called a *category*. As the reading "there exists a true proposition . . ." indicates, one of the categories is "true proposition" or "fact". But the existence of other readings of the existential prefix "there exists an x . . ." shows that

Conceptual Reference

the category "true proposition" is not indispensable in the theory of logic, for each *mode of significance* which can belong to the x of the existential prefix would give an alternative category, although such alternative categories, "thing", "particular", etc., may be taken as specifications of actuality which in a general way is describable as fact. The list of logical categories can be readily obtained from the divisions of type. This is because the mode of significance of a variable x is determined by the range of its values, and the latter depends upon the distribution of logical types within the context. Hence, in accordance with the simplified version of the theory of types given in the last Section of Chapter II, there are, besides the general category "fact", three *logical categories*: "particular", "predicate of particulars" (i.e. a predicate which has no structure), "predicate of predicates". Predicates of both types can be subdivided with respect to their mode of significance into "properties" and "relations".

Even a cursory examination of these logical categories will show that they differ in connotation, and that therefore the nature of each of them, as opposed to the others, can be clarified by description. Thus we might describe a particular as anything which has a unique occurrence in space and time. This is not incompatible with our previous assertion that categories are objectives for reference and have no function of describing or referring beyond themselves. Although connotative, they do not serve as means of description because they are not alienable from the connotation of the described object. If a category were given as a sole description of an object, the resulting proposition would be analytic or a tautology. If it were given in conjunction with other descriptive characteristics it could not enrich the import of the latter. For example, to describe a certain man as "an honest individual" is to say no more than that he is honest, for a being referred to as a man must be conceived of as a particular or individual being.

One might object to my theory of conceptual reference that it reintroduces the same difficulty which Russell's analysis of existential propositions meant to overcome. If one has conceded that the noun "man" in "Man exists" does not denote a particular person, it might seem, and for the same reason, that "proposition" in "there exists a proposition . . ." does not designate a single entity either. But the difference between the two cases is essential. There is no such thing as a generic man, but a proposition is a logical construction and as such it is a generic entity. Even when the objective for reference is "a proposition", it is not intended as the only one but as at least one entity without excluding the possibility of many propositions qualifying for the same description. This leaves an element of unanalysable generality at the very bottom of existential propositions, but nothing else should be expected after the rejection of the alternative theory which resolves general propositions into conjunctions or disjunctions of singular statements.

The function of conceptual reference in pure discourse, as outlined above, can be identified with the

Conceptual Reference

mode of significance, which I have called elsewhere "the claim to truth" of a proposition.* For a claim to truth means an assertion of the existence of a fact which the proposition expresses, and this is obviously the same thing as a statement of realization with regard to the corresponding conceptual complex. Thus to associate truth with the concept of "the intelligence of some men" is to assert that there is at least one fact, for example the fact of Plato's intelligence, through which the concept of human intelligence is realized.†

§ 3. Categories and Concepts

The list of logical categories is short: fact, proposition, particular, property of a particular, property of a property, relation, and, possibly, number.‡ But by specifying these logical categories

---

* Cf. my *Theory of Logic*, ch. i, Harper & Brothers, 1936.

† Since a judgment of perception (or a trivial existential judgment as well) has no conceptual reference from discourse to actuality, one might expect that it has no claim to truth either. This opinion is supported by the fact that such a judgment cannot be significantly contradicted. One might say that a perceptual judgment does not refer to a fact, but *presents* it. And this statement need not be taken as the idealist thesis that perception and perceptual judgment are indistinguishable. It is sufficient to hold that in the case of the perceptual judgment there is no fact mediating between it and the immediate presentation which is one of its constituents. It is still possible to distinguish between the immediacy of a perceptual presentation and the discursive conceptual nature of a judgment about it.

‡ Number is not a category, if, following Russell, we analyse it in terms of classes and relations. A class would be a redundant

with regard to various properties of space, time, or space-time combined, additional categories, to be called *ontological*, can be derived. For example, one transforms the logical category "particular" into the ontological category "substance" which expresses the temporal condition of continuity (or preservation of particularity) through change. Both sets of categories are conveniently grouped together because, in contrast with other concepts, they are not means of description. The addition of the category "particular" to a descriptive adjective does not increase the descriptive import of a proposition, so that "the table is brown" does not differ (descriptively) from "the table is a brown particular"; in the same manner the ontological categories lack any descriptive value. For example, "the invention of the airplane was an event of great military significance", a sentence in which the ontological category "event" is employed, is no better than "the invention of the airplane was of great military significance". There is another important property which distinguishes both kinds of categories from ordinary concepts: each category is *complementary* to the others within the same set. This means that a set of categories is a system in which, when some terms are given, the others can be inferred. Let the given category be "relation",

category in a logic based on the Principle of Extentionality. A further reduction of the number of categories is possible in a postulational logic. Thus in Curry's "logic without variables" function is the only logical entity, although it occurs with two modes of significance, as an operator or as an operand, depending on the place which it occupies in a row of symbols.

Conceptual Reference

and note that the medium of a relation is a proposition. Then one can infer that the other categories involved in the proposition are the category "particular" as exemplified by the related terms and the category "number", since there must be at least two terms. Similarly in the medium of space and time, the category "action" leads to the deduction of "substance", exemplified by the agent and the patient, and of "causation" as a correlation of change from the agent to the recipient.

The systematic correlations of categories must not be confused with an "intensional logic". The entertainment of one category does not generate of itself the thought of the others because it is psychologically possible to deal with some of them in complete disregard of their complementaries. An understanding of the request "Let us close our eyes and imagine *red*" converges upon the category of a property, exemplified by the colour "red", without involving the thought of a particular which may have this colour. Nor is there logical necessity for deduction of the complementaries from a given category, unless their system is already presupposed, as an additional premise, in the background of the deduction. If consideration of a relation symbolized by R makes one infer the existence of two particulars, this is because in the background of the consideration one has the propositional form $R(x, y)$ in which the distinction of significance between a relation and its terms is symbolically present. The deduction of complementaries to an ontological category is even more clearly dependent on the assumed background,

The Problems of Logic

in this case on empirical hypothesis about the nature of space and time. Thus if space and time are taken in separation from one another, the category "event" is understood as something which happens to an agent in its transaction with others and therefore its complementaries are "substance" and "causation". But within the theory of a combined space-time an event does not happen to a substance, it is itself an independent term in a network of time-like and space-like intervals, and zero-intervals. The choice among alternative sets of categories for a description of physical processes is not arbitrary or *a priori*, but is dictated by experiment and observation, and this alone is sufficient to bring out the difference between logical deduction and the transition from a category to its complementaries.

The contrast between categories and descriptive concepts must be understood in connection with an analysis of the nature of the latter. Consider the concept "man". As already noted it cannot designate a single entity, but has a contextual meaning. Thus within a proposition it is to be taken in the sense of "human particular", where "particular " is a logical category, but the adjective "human" remains to be explained. And so with other nouns, they are analysed into combinations of logical categories with descriptive adjectives. The adjectives themselves can be divided into two kinds, simple adjectives such as the property "red", and complex adjectives which are resolvable into conjunctions of simpler, if not simple, adjectives, as when "human" is defined by the conjunction "rational and animal".

Conceptual Reference

One can choose between two plausible theories of adjectives.

According to one theory, simple adjectives are *names* of simple qualities or sense-data. This would be entirely unobjectionable, if all simple adjectives were, like "black", in one-one correspondence with entirely specific qualities which have no variation of shades. But such an adjective as "red" designates a great many shades, and cannot be identified with an unambiguous name, since it is associated with "scarlet" in one mind, with "brick red" in another, and so forth *ad infinitum*. However, this objection is not conclusive to those who reject the widely spread assumption that sense-data and images are always specific. I, for one, believe, on the contrary, that presentations are very seldom, if ever, entirely specific. The evidence for the existence of indeterminate data, which to my mind is decisive, is the very common experience of making the original presentation more specific through concentration upon it. If it really becomes more specific, it must have originally been somewhat indeterminate. It will not do to say that the process under consideration is not a change in the specificity of the original datum, but a mere succession of different data, all equally determinate, but in an order of increasing intensity and complexity of detail. *As experienced* the process is a continuous transition of phases of specification within the same presentation, and not a mere replacement of one datum by another. Hence, if one is to trust his immediate experience, indeterminate data exist, and therefore adjectives can be used to name them without ambiguity. This would give a satisfactory account of adjectives, if complex adjectives could be treated as conjunctions of proper names for simple (although indeterminate) qualities. But, of course, a complex adjective such as "pie-bald", which is equivalent to the conjunction of simple adjectives "white and brown", is an exception. To take a more typical example, "human" is defined as "rational and animal", and the defining adjectives are themselves complex and definable in terms of other complex constituents, so that there is no hope of their ultimate resolution into simple adjectives, at least not into a finite number of such. But if this means that a complex adjective is not a name in the sense of the designation of a conjunction of a finite number of names of simple qualities, it does not follow that it cannot function as a name in some other sense. In this connection one must note a difference between simple and complex adjectives which is more important than their difference in "simplicity": while a simple adjective designates some quality of actual manifestations, a complex adjective stands for a *disposition* or potentiality of a manifestation. Hence, although not naming any realized property, a complex adjective can be taken as the unambiguous name of a unique disposition. For instance, "rational", unlike "red", does not designate a property of a sense-datum or of a memory-image, but it can name the capacity to act in a certain way under certain circumstances. One might think that the understanding of a disposition requires the formulation of a conditional ("If-

Conceptual Reference

then") proposition whose constituents are not less complex than the adjective in question. Thus if one interprets "A is rational" by some such proposition as "If confronted with a problem, A does not act impulsively, but weighs alternative means to a solution", then there is no doubt that the interpretation involves concepts of considerable complexity, viz. problem, reaction, act, impulse, etc. But I think that no conditional proposition is adequate to the predication of a disposition, although it can serve as a rule whereby the realization and therefore the inherence of a disposition can be tested. Thus let A be so stupid as to be undisturbed by problems. Then, of course, it would be false to say that "*A* is rational", but the corresponding conditional proposition (with the false antecedent "*A* is confronted with a problem") would be true. Notwithstanding this discrepancy in truth-value, the two statements are associated because the conditional form is used not as a proposition but as a rule of testing rationality, for example, as the following rule:

"To determine whether *A* is rational, see whether he can get around an obstacle placed in his way."

Since such a rule is not equivalent to the predication of a disposition, the choice of the rule to test the disposition is arbitrary within limits, and it would seem that these limits are flexible enough to allow for a prescription formulated exclusively in terms of simple adjectives and categories. For example, the rule to test rationality can be reformulated thus:

"To determine whether *A* is rational, find whether

The Problems of Logic

he can act upon another particular along some unopposed direction."

This formulation is illustrated in Fig. 1 by a spatial system of vectors, and the adequacy of the illustration proves that the corresponding conditional proposition is given exclusively in terms of spatial categories.

The "rational individual" is symbolized here by A, the opposing agent by B, the unopposed alternative way of acting upon B by the broken arrow. To take an interpretation of the scheme of Fig. 1,

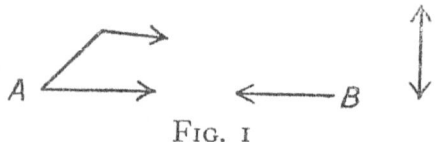

FIG. 1

let A be driving a car along a highway when he comes across an obstacle B—a sign "Danger! Road under construction". We should call A rational if, instead of forcing his way on, he takes a detour or decides upon some alternative course of action which can be symbolized by the broken arrow of Fig. 1. Of course, A's capacity of acting intelligently, which alone matters since the disposition is the same before and after the test, is left out of the picture. But if a spatial representation is at fault, so is any attempt to express dispositions in terms of actual manifestations or properties. And this can only mean that the word "capable", although not the name of a sensory quality such as "red", is just as ultimate and unanalysable and must be treated as one of the simple generic adjectives. To single out a particular dispo-

Conceptual Reference

sition one must give a name to the corresponding individual experience.

The alternative to the "name-theory" just explained is the contextual doctrine, according to which adjectives, like many other words, are contextual symbols, which contribute to the meaning of a sentence, but have no complete meaning of their own in isolation. We already admitted that class-terms or nouns, such as "man", are contextual symbols, and there is no reason to expect anything different from prepositions or from logical connectives; as Russell puts it "not even the most ardent Platonist would suppose that the perfect 'or' is laid up in heaven, and that the 'or's' here on earth are imperfect copies of the celestial archetype".* But an admission that some words do not stand for genuine constituents in a proposition is very different from the doctrine that no words do. Of course, there may be different versions of the contextual doctrine, but even in the very plausible form which it has taken in logical positivism it is not entirely flawless. The main flaw is the difficulty of determining which set of symbols can stand for a complete meaning or is a complete context. Usually every symbol short of a sentence is called incomplete, but not the sentence itself. Yet if a whole sentence is merely a string of marks, so are its constituent-words, and one can hardly understand why a longer string of marks is more capable of symbolizing a complete meaning than any of the shorter sets. Furthermore, if the meaning of a sentence consists in verifiability, which

* *Principles of Mathematics*, second edition, p. ix.

The Problems of Logic

is confirmation of its consequences, then it would seem that the original sentence to be meaningful also requires a context, viz. the context of the derivative sentences. And since derivation of consequences depends on the rules of transformation, one wonders whether anything except the whole language with its syntax can be a complete context.* But if this were so, a "vicious circle" of meanings would be inevitable. For let the meaning of a certain symbol or word A depend on its combinations with other words or symbols B, C, D, etc.; then the meanings of the latter would, among other things, depend on their combinations with A. As a way out of this difficulty one might suggest that the understanding of the meaning of a symbol (or word) is not an actual "rehearsal" of all its contextual combinations, but a *capacity* of the mind to perform correct linguistic formations and transformations which involve the symbol (or word) concerned.† As soon, however, as the contextualists admit "capacity", in some form or other, into the basis of language and meaning, their criticism of the "name-theory", to the effect that it involves reference to "hidden entities" such as disposition-properties, can be turned against their own theory.‡

* Cf. Reichenbach, *Experience and Prediction*, The University of Chicago Press, 1938. "So it may be said that only the rules of language confer meaning on a symbol" (p. 18).

† Cf. op. cit., p. 20, where it is said that the meaning of a word is its "capacity for occurring within meaningful sentences".

‡ A radical form of contextualism defines the meaning of words by the list (or, perhaps, by the speaker's capacity of supplying such a list) of legitimate combinations which they can take with one

Conceptual Reference

§ 4. Transcendental Logic

The theory of categories and concepts, outlined in §§ 2 and 3, is a revival, with essential differences,

another. The question is whether a legitimate combination is merely a formation in agreement with the syntax of language which is independent of considerations of truth. If it is, the contextualist account of meaning is inadequate. For, to take an example, there is nothing ungrammatical in "The cat is an animal flying over the North Pole", or even in "The cat is a machine flying over the North Pole", but such combinations of words, certainly, do not give the meaning of the word "cat". In short, a meaning cannot be given by combinations which are false propositions. And yet it is also true that we know the meaning of a word without professing to know the truth or falsehood of every combination into which it enters with other words. The usual explanation is that knowledge of the truth of a single combination, of a definition, is sufficient. For example, one does understand the meaning of the word "cat" if one knows that "the cat is a small furry carnivorous animal that can purr and mew", even if he believes that cats can fly over the North Pole. A definition is sufficient because it singles out the things defined, it applies to all of them and to nothing else. But a contextualist cannot have recourse to this ordinary theory of definitions. Thus he cannot define the word "cat" by means of combining it with "purring" and "mewing", because he cannot assume the understanding of these two verbs except in a context of combination with the word "cat". Furthermore, a definition is accepted only if it has the support of experience, and, certainly, not because of purely contextual considerations. A contextualist might disagree and argue for truth by convention or stipulation. But then he must choose between two alternatives: either only some truth, for example, the truth of definitions, is assigned by convention, or else there is a "wholesale" assignment of truth. The first alternative would put language in a constant danger of inconsistency, since a stipulated definition of a term may conflict with its established usage in true empirical propositions. The alternative of a "wholesale" assignment of truth is discussed in ch. v, § 4.

The Problems of Logic

of the transcendental logic. I agree with Kant that categories condition the *objective* character of empirical knowledge; I have expressed this by saying that the objective for reference in a proposition is a claim to truth, Kant by offering his transcendental logic as "a logic of truth".* Even our notational device for symbolizing the non-descriptive function of the objective reference is the same, in recommending the use of the individual-variable x I can refer to the following words of Kant: "It is easily seen that this object must be thought, only as something in general x, since outside our knowledge we have nothing which we could set over against this knowledge as corresponding to it."† Another important point of agreement with transcendental logic is the derivation of the list of categories from the modes of significance which propositions or judgments show. As Kant says: "This division (of categories) is developed systematically from a common principle, the faculty of judgment."‡ The reader will remember that I pointed out the systematic correlation of categories as complementaries of significance within the propositional form. Of course, the advance of logic since Kant has brought out a necessary revision in his list of categories, but the principle of their enumeration remains the same. Finally, my distinction between the categories of logic and the ontological categories as specifications (through the schemes of space and time) of the former is almost a replica of Kant's distinction between the categories

* *Kant's Critique of Pure Reason*, trans. by Norman Kemp Smith, Macmillan Co., p. 65.   † Ibid., p. 82.   ‡ Ibid., p. 72.

Conceptual Reference

and the schemata. Thus Kant writes: ". . . an application of the category to appearance becomes possible by means of the transcendental determination of time, which, as the schema of the concepts of understanding, mediates the subsumption of the appearances under the category".* And again: "The pure concept can find no object, and so can acquire no meaning which might yield a concept of some object. Substance, for instance, when the sensible determination of permanence is omitted, would mean simply a something which can be thought only as subject, never as a predicate of something else."†

There is, however, an essential difference between Kant and myself. I distinguish between categories used as objectives for reference and categories used as means of articulation of significance or organization of elements within a proposition. The same category may have both uses, even within the same thought. For example, in "The relation between them was friendship", the objective for reference is the category "relation" which is described as "friendship", therefore as "the relation of friendship", since friendship has the significance of a relation. The same category "relation" is used twice, first to be referred to, second to give the framework for the means of reference. The independence of the two uses of a category is proved whenever one takes the postulationalist position, for in a purely postulational treatment of logic there is complete abstraction from interpretation, i.e. from reference to

* *Kant's Critique of Pure Reason*, trans. by Norman Kemp Smith, Macmillan Co., p. 109. † Ibid., p. 113.

The Problems of Logic

objects outside the postulational discourse, and therefore all categories are used exclusively as molds of the distinctions of significance. To Kant the means of organizing thought in a proposition are identical with its objective character. He realized, of course, that the ways of organizing the elements of discourse may differ from the constitution of objects outside discourse, but instead of inferring, as he should have done, that the function of organizing thought must be distinct from the function of objective reference, he overlooked this in evolving his metaphysics of the contrasting of the phenomenal objectivity of categorical organization with things-in-themselves.

Hegel saw that a divorce between phenomenal and ontological objectivity is a camouflage for subjectivism, but in looking for a remedy he went to the extreme of identifying the development of discourse with the course of nature. In order to make this identification plausible he was forced to break the bonds between discourse and the calculus of propositions or judgments and to construe a system of categories not as derivative from the propositional form but as a *dialectic* in which one category emerges from another directly, without the medium of propositions, and therefore independently of the logic of consistency. Thus dialectic presupposes a critical attitude towards the importance of the propositional form:

"The thought, which is in our case the matter of sole importance, is only contained in the predicate: and hence the propositional form, like the subject . . ., is reduced to a meaningless phrase."*

* *The Logic of Hegel*, by William Wallace, Oxford, 1874, p. 85.

Conceptual Reference

Hegel's statement seems to mean this. The proposition, as it is treated in formal logic, allows only for an external relation between its terms, the subject and the predicate. But since the subject cannot be understood (unless from the preceding context) until it is described by the predicate, it follows that the whole content of the proposition is collected by the predicate and therefore the propositional form with its distinction between the terms is superfluous.

One might agree with Hegel that the propositional duality is unnecessary when thought proceeds as a development of categories because each category emerges from its predecessors by monopolizing the complete inventory of things in the world. If a category necessitates development into new categories, this is because as a framework for the totality of contents it proves to be inadequate: the contents overflow and the container cracks and must be replaced by one which serves better. And the "spot" where the old conceptual frame cracked gives the idea for the improvement and thus for the discovery of the succeeding category. Yet one might suspect that a procedure in which the totality of contents is compared with concepts in their order of increasing comprehensiveness would have to use propositions as means of comparison. Thus if we symbolize the totality of contents by T and the categories in the order in which they appear in Hegel's dialectic by C_1, C_2, C_3, etc., the dialectic might seem to be a succession of the propositions: T is C_1; T is C_2; T is C_3; and so forth. But this objection overlooks the fact that the

The Problems of Logic

totality of contents which becomes unfolded in the explicit series of categories, C_1, C_2, C_3, etc., is, prior to such an explication, given merely *implicitly* and so cannot be designated by a definite term T. In Hegel's own words "Being is the Notion, implicit only".* Hence the "identification" of "Being" with "Notion" is not to be taken literally as a statement of identity. Dialectic is replete with such "identifications" of categories and does not shrink from "self-contradiction" when the "identification" happens to be like the assertion that "Being is Nothing". The truth is that there would be a real contradiction only if "Being is Nothing" were a proposition. It is not: it is a symbolic expression for a process of thought which finds that "Being" and "Nothing" are *equally barren* explicit aspects of the underlying richness of potentialities.

If dialectic as a non-propositional logic is to be doubted, one must first discriminate. There is general doubt whether non-propositional thinking is possible, but this doubt seems to be gratuitous once it is understood that *creative thought*, thinking in the making, is different in kind from *expository thought* which gives an orderly form to the results of the creative process. While expository thought requires propositions as permanent, objective, and communicable records of discourse, creative thinking defies the propositional form because it is not an operation with identifiable terms but a growth of live ideas which are at first felt as mere germs of thought and later can branch out into divergent ramifications

* *The Logic of Hegel*, by William Wallace, Oxford, 1874, p. 84.

Conceptual Reference

within the main direction of the original impetus. If one's own psychological experience is to be trusted, Hegel's dialectic gives a close schema of the career of an idea undergoing the process of spontaneous transformations. But the psychological truth of a non-propositional thinking by its very self brings forward still another doubt, that of whether dialectic as a mental process has any right to claim to be a logic with a deductive necessity of transition from one category to another. Obviously Hegel's own triadic rhythm of categorial transition, from the "thesis" through the "antithesis" to the "synthesis", proved to be an inadequate method, since the resulting network of categories is not a system which cannot be rivalled by alternative constructions. But even if a more powerful method could be devised, the corresponding conceptual structure would have the convincing necessity of a work of art and not of a logical argument. A great work of art has, of course, its "logic". This is because as an organic whole it has an individuality which dictates the character of the detail, and the slightest attempt at alteration would strike at the form. But then the recognizing of the argument of a work of art is an unqualified submission to its individuality so that for a time one's own individuality as well as that of another work of art, are completely without the power to exist within one's conscious experience. Analogously, if we assume the individual frame of mind of a Hegel, we might feel the transition from "Being" through "Essence" to the "Idea" as a conceptual necessity. But we also might chose a different frame of mind

The Problems of Logic

and follow another line of imaginative conceptual development. However the similarity between dialectic and art is not close enough to attribute to the former the full aesthetic power of a composition. For in art the possibilities of imaginative digression are restricted by the necessity of conforming with the intrinsic order which belongs to the corresponding artistic medium of expression. For example, a musical composition must conform with the rules of harmony which are based upon the intrinsic order of the scale.* In a dialectical development, on the other hand, thought moves among abstractions which do not conform with the constitution of a particular medium of sense-data or images. It is true that even in dialectic there is a restrictive requirement to proceed towards a greater degree of specification. But it is doubtful whether this requirement determines a unique linear direction. Ordinarily specification is relative to a point of view, and when several alternative standpoints exist it seldom makes sense to say that one of them leads to a greater degree of specification than the others. Thus beginning with the most indeterminate category, C_1, "Being", one is not forced to proceed with C_2, C_3, etc., in the order in which Hegel introduces them, but, for some value of the subscript n, one can take as the next step either C_n or C_{n+1}, depending on one's interest and attitude. Moreover after a definite arrangement of categories is established, a new conceptual evaluation might necessitate a rearrangement. For according to Hegel himself, short of the "Absolute", everything

* Cf. D. Prall, *Aesthetic Analysis*, ch. i, 1936, Crowell Company.

Conceptual Reference

is in one sense more, and in another less, determinate than everything else. And, in giving preference to one of these senses, one must be guided by a feeling of its importance. The point is that expression of potentialities in concepts is always a matter of selection and therefore of personal emphasis; tendencies remain implicit until a mind, in building up its perspective on things, transforms some of them into a state of explicit distinctness or distinction. The choice of a "dialectic" is contingent on one's philosophy of value.

Chapter V

LOGIC AND REALITY

§ 1. Introduction

There is the question whether the forms of logic are embedded in the texture of experience outside discourse, in particular, whether the principles of logic have universal validity. Even within the domain of discourse the principles of logic have been challenged, but, although construction of alternative systems has lead to the discovery that the principle of the Excluded Middle can be superseded, no one has yet built a logic which is based on insignificance or inconsistency. Let logic be taken for a moment as a mere game; even so it must preserve distinctions of significance, the distinctions of type between functions and individuals, the discreteness of individuals, the difference between theorems and contingent formulas. If the necessity of non-contradiction in discourse is less obvious, if some writers claim that an alternative logic with the formula "$p \. \sim p$" as a postulate could be worked out, they overlook the fact that, whatever the relation between the principles of significance and of non-contradiction, without adherence to consistency there would be no assurance that the distinctions of significance have been preserved through the successive steps in the calculation. If in playing chess one would move the same figure at one time in the capacity of a bishop and at

Logic and Reality

another in the capacity of a knight, the game would break down through loss of its structure.

Any game would be unplayable if one could make even a single move arbitrarily endowing the figure to be moved with alternative capacities. Thus it appears that in a game as in discourse the principle of non-contradiction guarantees significance by bestowing recognizable distinctness to the various elements of the structure in order to prevent its disorganization.*

For, in the first place, the principle of non-contradiction gives expression to the "otherness" of the individual elements in discourse. Let x be such an element, then:

$$\sim (\exists x) : (x = x) . \sim (x = x).$$

The element x cannot be not itself and, therefore, it cannot be something other than itself. Next, func-

---

* The treatment of the principle of non-contradiction as a condition of significance does not mean that the denial of the principle, viz. "$p . \sim p$", is an insignificant statement; it means that if one conforms with this statement of contradiction one's discourse will lack significance. On the other hand, if the expression "$p . \sim p$" can be a significant statement, its formulation would presuppose the *use* of the principle of non-contradiction. For if one does not conform with the principle, nothing will prevent one from treating the symbol p as having a different significance in each of its occurrence, so that "$p . \sim p$" might become another way of writing "$p . \sim q$", which is not a statement of contradiction. The principle of non-contradiction, like any other principle, has the double function of rule and of statement. As a statement concerning the structure of discourse, it is true, even if it can be significantly denied; as a rule for carrying on an argument in discourse it is *indispensable*.

The Problems of Logic

tions (and, in particular, categories) can be distinguished from one another only as long as each has no significance other than its own. Thus if C is a certain category, then:

$$\sim (\exists\, C) : (C = C) \,.\, \sim (C = C).$$

Finally, the mutual exclusiveness of categories in discourse removes the possibility of an element to exemplify different categories; and this implies a third form of the principle of non-contradiction, a denial that the same element at once does and does not exemplify the same category (or, more generally, the same function):

$$\sim (\exists\, x) : C\,x \,.\, \sim C\,x.$$

These three forms of the principle of non-contradiction can be characterized as conditions of *notational and conceptual discreteness* which is indispensable for logical articulation, i.e. for the differentiation of one logical form from another.*

An extreme postulationalist might try to argue that abstract systems of logic do not require conceptual discreteness, while the condition of notational discreteness is satisfied as long as there is perceptual discrimination of one figure or mark on paper from

---

* The principle of non-contradiction can be treated as a definition of discreteness: "If there are discrete elements, then '$\sim (\exists x) \,.\, (f x \,.\, \sim f x)$'." In this, rather trivial, form the principle cannot be violated either in discourse or in experience outside discourse. For even if there were no discrete elements, the principle would be satisfied *vacuously*, it would be an implication which is true because of the falsehood of its antecedent.

Logic and Reality

another, which discrimination does not need the principle of non-contradiction. Identification of an approximate *perceptual discreteness* with notational discreteness is also held sufficient for the successful application of the rules of a calculus to the extent to which perceptual difference can be associated with the difference which symbols have in use. Take, for example, the formula of implication "$p \supset q$". While the intuitionalist insists on the distinction of conceptual significance between the proposition-variables and the logical constant symbolized by the horseshoe, an extreme postulationalist would be satisfied with a purely notational rule to the effect that of any three symbols in a row only one can be "$\supset$" and it must stand between the other two, which are small letters of the English alphabet. There would be no decisive consideration for either position, were it not for the identification of recurrent symbols, which the intuitionalist explains as so many exemplifications of the same concept, whereas the postulationalist is completely unable to explain it. Let the formula be:

(1) $\qquad p \supset . p \vee q.$

Perceptually the p's are two *distinct* marks; in order to construe them as a notational recurrence of the same symbol, perception must undergo a conceptual correction, for one must resort to interpretation. Similarity of shape is not sufficient for taking two marks to be the same symbol. Even "identical twins" are not mistaken for one person, and the numerical and positional distinctness of the twin p's cannot be disregarded. It is true that one can avoid

The Problems of Logic

the *physical* recurrence of the symbols p by the notational device of writing formula (1) in a new form as:

(2) $$\underset{p}{\overset{q}{>}} \dashrightarrow$$

But even this transcription cannot do away with *perceptual* recurrence, since the reading of the formula begins with a perception of p, then proceeds along the broken arrow, and ends with another perception of p, this time taken in disjunction with q. It may be true that the two percepts of p are identifiable as two representations or aspects of the same physical mark, but such an identification comes from a conceptual inference which goes beyond the discreteness of data in immediate perception.

The condition of conceptual discreteness of the basic elements of discourse is unqualified, unless we extend the term "discourse" to cover not only philosophy and science but also poems and other works of art. For if it is true that fine art does not aim at a "conceptual grasp" of things, but at an insight which is gained through a display of images and emotion, it is likely that the artistic function of sentences is essentially contextual; they are not isolatable complete meanings with a definite categorial structure, but rather "transient" carriers of a developing idea whose adequate expression is in the work of art taken as a whole.

It may happen that the same sentence is used in some treatise and in a literary essay, but then they do not convey the same proposition. In art the sen-

Logic and Reality

tence need not express any proposition at all; it has the *functional* significance of contributing to the momentum of the growing aesthetic experience of the reader, but when left behind it does not leave the same trace with an identical logical structure on all readers' minds. If the work of art is powerfully coherent it does not matter that the sentence already read arouses in some people fanciful or irrelevant responses; subsequent sentences will correct the momentary aberrations by the weight of the accumulating co-ordination of ideas and feelings. The division of the essay into sentences does not correspond to the divisions in the rhythm of its artistic thought, nor is the pulsation of the latter translatable into a series of clear-cut, discrete terms; transformations and ramifications of a live idea, as contrasted with mere conceptional exposition and demonstration, are fused into an organic unity. It was already pointed out that because of the organic unity transition from one phase to another within a great work of art has a necessity which is similar to the logical necessity in deduction, except for the fact that as one leaves one work of art for the experience of another one may recognize the elements of the former in a new composition of the latter and therefore in an *alternative* way of necessary transition. Now we are in a position to make an amendment. What one might mistake for the same element, for example, for the same sentence, in two distinct compositions, conceals in reality two different contributions since the functional significance of a sentence in two different contexts of feeling and imagery cannot be the same. It remains true that the "logic" of a work of art is grounded in its individuality, since it is the "logic" of an individual organism, but this individuality is now seen to be akin to the universality of formal logic, because, like the latter, it allows for no competition, although the grounds of universality are utterly different in the two cases. While logic proceeds from discrete premises to discrete conclusions and can have universal validity only in virtue of this discreteness, art is a "sublimation" of discreteness and its universality is the impossibility of identifying its content with isolatable means of expression. Even in music, where it may appear that the experience of a listener is punctuated into discrete units corresponding to the notes of the score, there is in reality a continuous shift of perspectives upon the same musical structure, and the emergence of a "perspective" does not coincide with the single tone which happens to be struck at the time. If elements in a work of art are discernible, this is a discrimination of *values*, which, even in standing out against one another, never lose their contextual interconnection and therefore never attain the prominence of conceptual segregation, which would be destructive of organic unity. If this is true, the discourse of art does not conform with the principle of non-contradiction taken as the condition of conceptual discreteness.

If discourse in art can be conceptually indiscrete and, therefore, not subject to the principle of non-contradiction, one can easily imagine experience outside discourse to be entirely independent of

Logic and Reality

logic.* Indeed, metaphysicians and artists as well as "common-sense" people have often described reality as a continuum of blending sensations and emotions; yet it is equally true that the continuum of experience is a background against which manifestations are detached which are nearly discrete to perception and entirely so in conceptual analysis.

However, it is not necessary to appeal to the evidence of actual experience, it is sufficient to show, as in § 2 of this chapter, that a continuum *can* be analysed into discrete elements; and this is sufficient not for any ulterior purpose of metaphysics, but in order to establish the bearing of the principle of non-contradiction upon experience outside discourse even if the latter is assumed to be and, in fact, happens to be a continuum. At first one would think that where there are no discrete elements, no x's, the principle that "$\sim (\exists x) . (fx . \sim fx)$" cannot have application, although vacuously it would still be true. But we shall see that in what will be called a continuum of adjectival indeterminacy the discrete x's exist; and even where there is no discreteness,

* There are writers who argue that one cannot discuss within the syntax of discourse anything with a different syntax, just as it would be senseless to talk in English, with the resources of English alone, of sentences which have an un-English formation. To this one can answer that the distinction between the theory of logic and the exhibition of logical forms allows for a discussion of forms which are different from the principles which lead the discussion. Furthermore, we do not propose to discuss an "illogical" situation in the sense of a structure incomparable with the principle of non-contradiction, but only as something entirely *amorphous*, without even excluding its disposition for acquiring logical form.

The Problems of Logic

there is always a *disposition* for actualization, the emergence of entities of different degrees of discreteness. It is true that the continuum of experience does not mean that "there are distinct actual entities", but it means that "distinct entities are realizable", and consideration of "would-be entities" is subject to the principle of non-contradiction as much as discussion of discrete existents. Of course, to describe a continuum in terms of emerging actualities is already a conceptual analysis, but this cannot be helped since we must understand the nature of dispositions through their outcome in manifestations. To be more precise, the principle of non-contradiction, although not descriptive of a continuum in its state of pure potentiality, is a *rule* in agreement with which actualization must take place. But although a rule, it is also more than that if one takes a rule to be a regulation which allows for modification or even for an alternative. There can be no actualization except as specification towards complete determinacy of discreteness; as an expression of the universal logic of actualization the principle of non-contradiction has universal application and validity.

§ 2. Continuity and Indeterminacy

The principle of non-contradiction "$\sim (\exists x): \phi x . \sim \phi x$", taken as a *description* of actuality outside discourse, might fail for two reasons, irrelevancy and falsehood. This is so because with reference to actuality the significance of "x" and "ϕ" is different, the first is a symbol for a particular, the second for a

Logic and Reality

characteristic, and corresponding to this difference in significance two kinds of non-discreteness or continuity are conceivable. There is the possibility of a substantival homogeneous medium with no particulars standing out against one another so that one could not single out "this" in distinction from "that". In such a medium there would be nothing designatable as an "x" and the principle of non-contradiction, although true vacuously, would have no positive bearing on the situation. From this *substantival continuity* we shall distinguish *adjectival indeterminacy*. Suppose we have singled out a particular x, but are unable to decide whether it has or lacks the predicate ϕ. Under the circumstances x would have no discrete character, and two particulars x and y without discrete characters would be descriptively indistinguishable from each other. In the face of such indeterminacy the principle of non-contradiction might appear to be false. But let us consider both kinds of non-discreteness in some detail.

To begin with illustrations, let us exemplify discrete particulars by three dots in a row:

. . .

They are discrete and stand out against the background because of the gaps between them. By contrast, there is continuity if the gaps are filled up; but if they are, the individual points vanish, being fused into a line:

―――

Of course, one may still argue that the line is made of particular points. But if we mean by a line, as we

The Problems of Logic

shall in this discussion, a line as it is perceived, then we obviously do not perceive any point on a line, until we single out one by intersecting the given line with another. If the "actualization" of a point by intersection encourages one to say that it is a "discovery" of a point which had been there all the time, he must hold that there are points on a line which while not actually perceived are perceivable. This view would enable one to interpret the continuum of a line in terms of discrete points by asserting that the gap between any two perceived points is filled by perceivable points. To make the assertion precise, one can translate it into the system of postulates for the mathematical continuum if one interprets the symbol "$<$" as the relation "to the left of" and the designation "element" as " a point on a line":

(1) Given a class of elements K, if a and b are not the same elements of K, then either $a < b$ or $b < a$;

(2) Given a class of elements K, if $a < b$, then a and b are not the same elements of K;

(3) Given that a, b, c, are elements of K, if $a < b$ and $b < c$, then $a < c$;

(4) Given a class of elements K, if $a < b$, then there exists an element c such that $a < c$ and $c < b$.

(5) If every element of the class K belongs to one of its sub-classes K_1 and K_2, and if every element of K_1 stands on the left-hand side of "$<$" in relation to every element of K, then there exists an element c in K such that (a) every element which is on the left-

Logic and Reality

hand side of "$<$" with relation to c belongs to K_1, and (*b*) every element which is on the right-hand side of "$<$" with relation to c belongs to K_2.

The postulate (4) is the "density" postulate which leaves no gaps in a series of elements arranged according to the five postulates. Since its ruling is that there always is an element between any two given elements, this postulate requires "the existence of an infinite number of elements", provided the existence of at least two of them is ascertained.

Now the doubt whether postulate (4) can be interpreted in terms of discrete points depends on the phrase "the existence of an infinite number of elements". If the existence of a point means its presence in perception, then there exists only a finite number of points, for intersections of the given line can exhibit points only at a finite distance from one another. As soon as one tries to imagine contiguous lines of intersection, one obtains the picture of compactness which is not punctuated by discernible points. The falsehood of postulate (4) in this interpretation is accompanied by the trivial or "vacuous" truth of the principle of non-contradiction in its application to points on the line-interval between any two given points.* If, however, we follow the sugges-

* So far as the space of perception is concerned, I have no objection to the existence of points taken literally as extensionless and indivisible entities. As I look at one of the corners of this page, I see at the intersection of the edges something which I am unable to imagine (in the sense of being unable to form an image) as either reducible in size or divisible.

tion at the end of § 1 and interpret the principle of non-contradiction as a rule, i.e. as a statement of a condition under which a certain potentiality is actualized, then not only the principle is not trivial but it discloses the way to another interpretation of "the existence of points on a line", which was anticipated in the words "perceivable although not perceived". It would be more accurate to speak of potentiality for perception of points, but whatever expression is used, the postulate (4) is true if it is taken as the statement that one *can* "actualize" a point on the interval between any two actual points. The existence of an infinite number of points which the postulate requires is then not to be understood as the existence of actual points but as an unrestricted potentiality for the emergence of new points. The line itself or any other substantival homogeneous medium exhibiting a disposition to be organized by the rules of non-contradiction, e.g. the mathematical continuum, can be called, by analogy with such a generic percept as given by a red patch, a determinable entity. The specification of a generic entity may be incapable of completion, for example, description of points discernible on a line is never final, nevertheless it can be carried on with a growing accumulation of detail, and therefore the determinable entity is not indeterminate. This marks an important difference between a substantival continuum and an adjectival absence of discreteness, to which must be added the further distinction that an "adjectival continuum" is not amenable to treatment by the postulates (1), (2), (3), (4), and

Logic and Reality

(5), and that it "endangers" the principle of non-contradiction itself.

To illustrate the adjectival continuum in a perceptual field let us take the perception of colours which shade off into one another, say, of red changing into orange. To emphasize the continuity of change one says that one colour changes into the other imperceptibly, although the transition is within the percept. The fact that the transition is imperceptible explains why it cannot be described or treated by the postulates for the mathematical continuum: while the postulates require discrete elements, there is no basis for the separation of one shade from another as two discrete data. Any boundary would be an arbitrary line of demarcation and in order to be perceivable it would have to be in some colour which contrasts with the background against which it is drawn; consequently the presence of the boundary would be an alteration in the very property of imperceptible change in the original percept under consideration. Nor is it possible to conceive the colours shading off into each other to be composed of breadthless perceivable (although not perceived) bands each having a unique specific shade of colour, even if this shade is very similar to the shades of colour of the bands in the immediate neighbourhood. Even if a breadthless band were perceivable, it would appear colourless, since in perception colour always entails extension. It is not easy to describe exactly what one perceives, but I think this much will be granted: there exists a region in the percept which would be unhesitatingly recognized as red and another as orange, however many variations of shade each of them contains, but between these two regions there lies a fringe of transition which could not be classified as either red or not-red, nor as either orange or not-orange. It is here that one can challenge the principle of non-contradiction. Let the fringe of transition be designated by "x" and "red" by "f". Then we have:

$$(\exists x) . [\sim fx . \sim (\sim fx)].$$

This is a denial of the principle of non-contradiction, at least if the principle of double negation "$p . \equiv . \sim (\sim p)$" holds good. Hence it appears that in order to rescue the principle one must abandon the formula and join the mathematical intuitionists who have their own reason for denying that the implication of p by $\sim \sim p$ is not a theorem (which denial is another way of saying that the principle of the excluded middle "$\sim p \lor p$", although not a falsehood, is not a theorem). One might object to the procedure of adapting an alternative logic, such as the logic of mathematical intuitionism, as arbitrary and incompatible with the intuitionalist position that no formula of logic which is ascertained by intuition to be a validating form can be suspended in its operation even if its suspension is required to uphold another principle. This objection leads to the more general question of the status of alternative logics.

Alternative logics are related to one another as much as euclidean geometry is related to the non-euclidean varieties; i.e. as postulated systems they

Logic and Reality

are all on a par; each system is internally consistent, and while it seems that one of them rejects the same principle which another accepts, this misleading appearance is explained away by showing that the two systems may use the same sentence, but in each of them this sentence stands for a different principle. Thus while "The sum of angles of a triangle is 2 d" is true in Euclid and false in some non-euclidean geometries, there is no real disagreement because the word "triangle" does not mean the same thing in the alternative systems of geometry. Likewise in rejecting the formula "$p \lor \sim p$" the three-value logic does not contradict aristotelean logic, because this formula must change its logical significance with the change in the number of truth-values attributable to the constituent proposition-variables.

The situation becomes quite different when one turns from abstract systems to their interpretations. A region of physical space cannot exemplify at once a euclidean and a riemannian structure; and the question which of the two is exemplified must be determined by measurement and observation. Similarly an empirical statement such as "Princeton is a University town in New Jersey" has a definite number of truth-values and therefore must be treated by the logic which allows for just that number of truth-values. Thus the logic of actual discourse is determined in exclusion of alternative systems by taking into consideration formal properties which belong to empirical statements. On the other hand, to complete the analogy with geometry, one must observe that alternative systems of geometry may

The Problems of Logic

be incompatible as describing the same region of physical space and yet have a joint application by referring each to a different region; for example, while regions where matter is present are "curved", at a great distance from matter space flattens into a practically euclidean state. An analogous application of alternative logics to co-exclusive groups of statements has been practised by the intuitionists in mathematics; Brouwer adheres to the principle of the excluded middle in dealing with finite collections and suspends its operation in infinite domains. If infinity is taken as a restriction upon specification of elements by enumeration, one can treat it as a case of indeterminacy and generalize Brouwer's position, in accordance with the argument of this section, by restricting the competence of the principle of the excluded middle to statements about actual or determinable discrete entities as contrasted with statements of adjectival indeterminacy. However, this course is not necessary: instead of dividing statements into two groups, one might prefer to *define* a proposition as a statement the truth or falsehood of which is decidable, and then proceed with a suspension of the principle of the excluded middle whenever one *cannot* decide whether a statement itself is true on the ground that neither the statement itself nor its contradictory is a meaningful proposition assignable as a value to the variable in the formula "$p \lor \sim p$". The intuition that "$p \lor \sim p$" is a validating form arises only in dealing with decidable propositions in actual discourse; when, as in complete abstraction of structure from actual argument, the

Logic and Reality

grounds for decision are withdrawn, the outcome is indeterminacy in which intuition is no longer operative.*

* In this Section I have made some use of Mr. Max Black's article "Vagueness" (*Philosophy of Science*, Vol. 4, No. 4, 1937), but I do not follow him in his "operationalist" procedure, and my idiom is entirely realist, so that I prefer to discuss "indeterminate qualities" where he speaks of "vague symbols".

According to Mr. Black, a word, such as "red", is said to be vague when an observer hesitates whether it should be applied to a given object. Such hesitation, and, therefore, vagueness of a word W can be measured by the ratio of the number m of decisions to apply it to an object O to the number n of decisions against application. Thus corresponding to any vague W there exists a *definite function* C (W, O), called the consistency of application of W to O, which is the limit of the ratio $\frac{m}{n}$, when the number of decisions concerning the application of the word is indefinitely increased. It follows that linguistic vagueness can be eliminated by the use of a language in which the vague W's are replaced, with a suitable modification of context, by the C-functions; in particular, while the principle of the excluded middle is invalid with regard to the assertion "O is W", it is restored through the replacement of "O is W" by "W (O, C)", i.e. "O is W with the consistency of application C" in the form: either W (O, C) or $W\left(O, \frac{1}{C}\right)$.

This interesting procedure, being limited to linguistic behaviour, does not account for the frequent cases when there is no ratio $\frac{m}{n}$ because hesitation in characterizing an object prevents one from making a verbal decision. When observers are not sure whether the datum is red or not-red, they often suspend judgment. Also repetition of verbal decisions is ruled out whenever the datum to be characterized is an irrepeatable event.

The Problems of Logic

§ 3. Logical Form

It is a common opinion that logical form can be shown and discussed in complete abstraction from actual discourse. "We get the picture of the pure form if we abstract from the meaning of the single words, or symbols (so far as they have independent meanings). That is to say, if we substitute variables for the constants of the proposition."* The difficulty with this opinion is that in abstraction from the meaning of words a form cannot be called *the* form of a proposition because it can be reformulated with an endless variation of a more or less specific expression. For example, let the abstract expression be "$p \supset q$". More generically it can be given as "$f_1(p)$", or "$f_2(q)$" or "$f_3(p, q)$"; but it can also be specified as "$(m \lor n) \supset q$", and so forth. Dissociated from actual statements these expressions do not have arguments with a definite structure; hence each can represent propositions of such different forms as "If to-day is Friday, to-morrow is Saturday", "Either there will be a world-war or dictatorship will replace democracies implies that we live in an age of decadence", and so on. This variability is one of the reasons why the intuitionalist must insist that formal logic is the logic of actual discourse, and that unless intuition of logical form deals with the propositions in which the forms are embedded, it would be a vain pursuit of the evasive.† But as soon as one decides to look for

* L. Wittgenstein, *Logical Form*, Arist. Society, Suppl. vol. ix.

† Wittgenstein himself, and in the same paper, is forced to recognize that the study of form cannot proceed *a priori*, but must depend on considerations of the subject-matter, as when one finds that the

Logic and Reality

the forms of propositions in actual discourse, he is confronted with the difficult problem of the relation which logical form has to linguistic syntax and to ontological structure. In approaching this problem by means of a comparatively simple case, illustrated in Fig. 1, I shall begin with a notational convention of using a sentence in quotation marks to designate the sentence, the same sentence without quotation marks in discussing the corresponding proposition, and the same sentence italicized to distinguish the fact from the proposition.

FIG. 1

Thus a distinction is to be made between the sentence "The short bar crosses the long bar" and the true proposition which it expresses, viz. The short bar crosses the long bar, which is true because of the fact that *The short bar crosses the long bar*. Whether or not the proposition and the fact have the same form depends on what is meant by the fact.

truth-table for the propositions "a is red" and "a is blue" gives only three truth-possibilities, since the "*a priori*" possibility TT" is excluded by the subject-matter of the propositions concerned. Furthermore, if the form is to show formal properties, "$a R b$" is not the form of "a hates b", because it does not show that "to hate" is a non-reflexive, non-symmetric, and non-transitive relation.

The Problems of Logic

If the fact is the perceptual image of Fig. 1, then it is a single event of a certain pattern which is capable of being conceptually analysed in many different ways. We can say: The pattern of Fig. 1 is a picture of a window; There are two squares and two rectangles; There is a cross in a rectangular frame; The short bar crosses the long bar; The short bar is one inch distant from the bottom; and so forth. All these correct descriptions differ in form and therefore *none* has *the* structure of the perceptual event. Nor is the latter given by the conjunction of all true propositions about Fig. 1, because the original event *as perceived* can never give so much information. When I first glanced at Fig. 1, I did not see it either as a window or as two squares on top of two rectangles, and although I now recognize the truth of these descriptions, the recognition merely shows that the original percept had presented a *potentiality* for alternative descriptive analyses, which may be called alternative *conceptualizations*. Now if such a conceptualization, when correct, is to be called a fact, this gives another sense to the word, and then there is no difference between a fact and a true proposition. An attempt to find a difference in the utmost specificity of a fact as contrasted with a more or less generic description given by propositions is unsuccessful when it comes to percepts which are either determinable without ever yielding to a completely specific account or else intrinsically indeterminate. Nor are facts to be postulated as "indispensable grounds" for the truth of propositions, since perceptual events together with their potentialities for

Logic and Reality

conceptualization would seem to take complete care of verification or justification of empirical propositions. If one wonders how a description of actuality can be justified by reference to potentiality, one must understand that through the description potentiality has been actualized in certain concepts. With regard to an object of description as it was prior to conceptualization a true proposition is not a report about its structure but rather a rule whereby it can be organized into a conceptual structure.* Logical form is conceptual. This means that a proposition is true when it provides concepts which can be traced back to the original percept as realizing its tendency to acquire a certain organization. Organization of percepts comes through perceptual discernment, but discernment is often guided by conception. There was a time when magazines amused their readers with puzzle-pictures. You would look, for example, at a picture of an ordinary tree, but the caption underneath "Where is the cat?" would make you

---

* The treatment of an empirical proposition as a rule for conceptualization does not imply, as the pragmatists and logical positivists would have it, that the sole meaning of a proposition is its verification. A proposition often refers to a present or a past percept; if it does, the question whether it is a correct conceptualization is decided immediately, i.e. in the process of conceptualization itself and not by means of some future act of verification. The relation of conceptualization to a percept, which is a relation of actualization to potentiality, is unique in kind and is not based on recognition of resemblance, whereas the emphasis on verification suggests the false opinion that one recognizes in experience the features anticipated in a proposition, that there is a "country-map" relationship between the two.

The Problems of Logic

turn the picture through many angles until the figure of a cat would emerge from the outline of branches and leaves. If you ask whether it is true that the figure of the cat was in the picture before it was found there, the answer is rather no; without the caption as a conceptual guide for perceptual organization, the prerequisite discernment might never take place; there would be a picture of a tree with merely a disposition or tendency for the emergence of the figure of a cat. Any descriptive proposition, like the captions of puzzle-pictures, suggests a certain way of looking at and of seeing things; the truth of description is, therefore, not correspondence, by duplication in a proposition, to an already existent objective structure, but correspondence in the sense of *adequacy* in conceptualization. We need not, then, duplicate a proposition by italicizing it and calling the italicized duplicate a fact; but it would seem that we cannot dispense with quotation marks and identify the form of a sentence with the form of the corresponding proposition.

The discrepancy between the sentential and the propositional forms is a commonplace to anyone who speaks different languages, as when he finds that the English "It is cold" and the Russian "Holodno", although unlike in their linguistic structure, express the same proposition and therefore must have the same conceptual form. But even within one language the same proposition can be expressed by sentences which differ in form, even to the extent of giving an appearance of contradiction, as Mr. C. A. Lloyd demonstrates in this striking example:

Logic and Reality

> I cannot but think you are mistaken;
> I can but think you are mistaken.*

Of course, knowledge of idioms and linguistic conventions is indispensable in telling which sentences are identifiable in spite of structural differences, and which of them are superior in directness and adequacy of expression; yet this knowledge is only the first step towards an understanding of the relationship between linguistic and conceptual form. Let the given sentence be a direct and adequate expression of a proposition; this does not mean that the two show an identical structure but only that they have certain formal properties in common. A sentence and a proposition are both *expressions*—a sentence expresses a proposition by verbalizing or symbolizing it, a proposition expresses perceptual experience by conceptualizing it—and both have a *multiplicity* of constituents which are arranged in some *order*. Linguistic structure would be entirely adequate if and only if it had the same multiplicity and the same order as the corresponding propositional form. But the spatial series of written words or the temporal sequences when they are read aloud, which make up the order in a sentence, is not the same thing as the order of subordination or co-ordination of concepts within the proposition. Thus when we understand that in Fig. 1 "the short line crosses the long line", we must not think first of the short line, the next moment of the relation of crossing, and finally of the long line, but we must

---

* *We who speak English*, p. 74, 1938, Crowell Co., N.Y.

The Problems of Logic

conceive of the relationship *together* with its terms. Conceptual organization takes place *at once* as an expression of the complementary logical significance in which the constituents of a proposition stand to one another. Mere words and symbols as marks on paper or vibrations of the air, belong to the same logical type and therefore cannot show an organization with distinctions of the order of significance. Turning to multiplicity, the question whether the constituents of the sentence can be set in one-one correspondence with the constituents of the proposition, is, as a rule, answered in the negative if the constituents of the sentence are taken to be single words. But there may only seem to be inadequacy when several words cluster together into a single phrase or expression which can be counted as one constituent, with a reduction in multiplicity as a result. For example, the grammatical function of the article "the" in the sentence "the short line crosses the long line" is to collect into one constituent the words "the short line" and into another "the long line", and with the verb "crosses" this gives three linguistic constituents to be set in one-one correspondence with a certain conceptualization of the percept of Fig. 1. But even when words are thus collected into groups, one cannot determine whether the sentential and the propositional multiplicity is the same unless he is sure that each group of words stands for a single object of conception. Russell, for one, has denied that a phrase such as "the short line", a phrase of the form "the so-and-so", which he called a "definite description", can ever stand for a single

Logic and Reality

constituent in a proposition.* And there certainly are many examples of propositions in which no constituents corresponding to the definite descriptions of the sentences can be found. Thus if we accept the truth of the proposition expressed by the sentence "The devil does not exist", we must, to avoid self-contradiction, deny that "the devil" designates a single "objective for conceptual reference". The proposition is not about the devil, since if it were, such an individual would exist; nor is it about the concept of a devil, for to deny the existence of such a concept would be untrue. We might say that the definite description does not describe a single entity where there is nothing present which can be named or labelled or referred to by such a demonstrative symbol as "this"; but then we should expect that when a definite description can be replaced by a name, there is a corresponding constituent within the proposition.† Thus, while recognizing the difference between names and descriptions, we might argue that in the statement "The man in the iron mask was Molière," "the man in the iron mask" describes that particular constituent whose name was Molière. Or, to refer again to Fig. 1, "the short line" and "the long line" would seem to stand for perceptual lines since the latter could be labelled, say, as "a" and "b". Against this Russell might object that in the absence of a percept it cannot be named and yet its description within a proposition retains the same meaning as when the

* Cf. the footnote on p. 126.
† This, I believe, is the view of G. E. Moore and his school.

percept was present. It may well be that "the man in the iron mask" is nothing but a legend, this possibility does not affect the meaning of "The man in the iron mask was Molière". On the other hand, if we qualify by saying that, since logical distinctions do not depend on the empirical observation of existence it is not actual naming but a consideration of what is in principle nameable that matters, we should be in a position to formulate a criterion of "nameability". For an attempt, we might say that if a sentence has the form "f—" where "f" represents a genuine constituent of a proposition and "—" symbolizes a definite description, then the definite description is in principle replaceable by a name. According to this criterion "the short line" in "the short line crosses b" is replaceable by the name "a" because the verb "crosses" and the name "b" are known to designate real constituents of a conceptualized percept. Also "the man in the iron mask", as this occurs in the above sentence about Molière, is replaceable by a name, even if the man in question was not Molière, or even if there were no such man at all. The issue is partly a question of the foundations of logical analysis. Therefore one might side with Russell against the admission of different *uses* of a definite description in different contexts on the general ground that this admission runs contrary to the uniformity of an analytic procedure and will lead to criteria which have the character of *ad hoc* rules. Without professing to give a complete account of the principles of logical analysis, I shall make a few comments which appear to be sound and throw

Logic and Reality

some additional light on the function of definite descriptions.

The terms of logical analysis must be the elements of logic, i.e. analysis is a procedure which ends in the replacement of the original sentence to be analysed by a sentence given entirely in terms which are recognized in the theory of logic as the *basic logical forms*. The basic forms of modern logic, if we limit ourselves to non-compound propositions, are existential and non-existential general proposition-structures. Hence if we can, and this is exactly what Russell has done, translate a singular sentence, i.e. a sentence about a definite description, into a combination of existential and non-existential statements in which no trace of the definite description is left, our translation conforms with the requirement of logical analysis. And further points as to the number of the component statements of each kind, of their structure and mode of combination is guided by a consideration of the properties of significance which are attributable to the original sentence to be analysed. Thus the multiplicity of component-statements in the analysis of a singular proposition could be reduced if one disagrees with Russell and takes "number" to be categorially as ultimate as "predicate" or "particular". While Russell analyses "The short line crosses b" into "There exists an x which is short and linear and there is no y, other than x, which is short and linear, and it is false that there exists an x which is short and linear but does not cross "b", the recognition of "number" as a category would give some such

The Problems of Logic

simplified analysis as "There exists an x such that it alone is short and linear and such that it crosses b". Once the multiplicity of the components is established, their structure may usually be found through the segregation of the logical objectives for reference from the descriptive constituents. In the analysis of a singular proposition the objective for reference is picked out by the category of the particular, and is then symbolized by the individual-variable.* But if logical categories are to be used in the exhibition of form, one must have recourse to the theory of logic where they are introduced by means of definite descriptions in such statements as "The particular is a logical category". Now these statements are obviously not amenable to Russell's treatment. We cannot translate "The particular is a logical category" into "There exists an x such that it is particular etc.", because if x were particular it could not be "the particular" in the sense of "the category of particularity", and also because the very use of an

---

* The identification of the objective for reference, within a singular proposition, with a particular allows for a uniform treatment of definite descriptions regardless of whether they describe anything or not. "The short line which crosses b in Fig. 1" ... is about a particular, and so is "the man in the moon . . .", but the former gives a correct description of one particular, whereas the latter gives a false description of what it refers to; no particular is a man in the moon. On the other hand, the theory that definite descriptions are the constituents of a proposition when they are in principle replaceable by names cannot explain what a proposition is about when its descriptive phrase does not describe anything. We can say that "the man in the moon" ... is about a particular because particulars exist, but we cannot say that it is about the man in the moon, since there is no such man.

individual-variable such as *x* presupposes an understanding of its categorial significance and therefore of the fact that the particular is a logical category. It follows that a definite description of a category forms an exception to Russell's theory of descriptions: it is unanalysable and it stands for a single and isolatable conceptual entity. Of course, Russell's definite descriptions are meant to be descriptions of individuals, and not of universals or class-terms, as in the statement "The triangle is a geometrical figure". Yet I do not wish to subscribe to an identification of categories with ordinary universals. While a category is a single and ultimate concept, the possibility of reformulating "The triangle is a geometrical figure" into "All triangles are geometrical figures", without any loss of meaning, makes it very doubtful whether such universal-words as "triangle" ever stand for genuine constituents in propositions. Also ordinary universal-words suggest "objects" of a peculiar kind, so that a Platonic realm of ideas or a neo-realist subsistence is only a natural development of this suggestion. But categories do not involve metaphysical hypostatization, because they stand for distinct *functions* in a logical context, rather than for objects. Even "the objective for reference" is not an object but the mode of significance in the idea of a counterpart to the function of referring to or describing something within a proposition.

§ 4. LOGIC BY CONVENTION

To say that categories are not subsistent entities, but distinct conceptual functions to organize the

The Problems of Logic

subject-matter within the context of a proposition; that the form of a proposition itself is not a replica of a structure outside discourse, but a mode for conceptualizing experience; and that the principles of logic are the rules for such modes of conceptualization—is to propose a moderate functional theory of logical form. It must not be confused with the radical functional theory, to be called the operational theory of form, which rejects logical intuition in favour of convention by proclaiming the following theses:

(1) The elements of a sentence or a proposition do not represent the elements of its subject-matter. The relation between a sentence or a proposition and its subject-matter is not a "map-country" relationship recognizable by intuitive inspection;

(2) The elements of a sentence or a proposition have no meaning in isolation from the context of discourse;

(3) Sentences or propositions do not describe; they are means to deal with, to determine, or organize a situation. They are neither true nor false, but are accepted or rejected by convention according to their efficiency in coping with a situation: they are conventional rules or prescriptions;

(4) Logical "theorems" are also rules by convention. They are distinguished from empirical

Logic and Reality

"propositions" which have a limited range of application because they are found to be efficient in any field.

An appraisal of the first thesis from the standpoint of my moderate functional theory is given in § 3; in brief it amounts to this. If the subject-matter of a proposition is a fact in the sense of descriptive conceptualization of experience, then the proposition and the fact are identical and their elements are the same. If the subject-matter is a fact in the sense of a situation outside discourse, then its elements, if it has any, are not duplicated by the elements of a proposition. But even in this case the elements of a true proposition *express* real tendencies of a situation and the question of the adequacy of such an expression is decided by intuition.

With regard to the dependence of meaning on context my position is that categories and simple adjectives have a relative independence, to the extent to which each functions in a constant way of its own, i.e. contributes the same unique conceptual import when transferred from one context to another. Furthermore, while a constituent which is not a proposition may require the context of a proposition (or of a propositional function or of a rule) towards the completion of which it is a contribution, I do not believe that this context must be expanded until it coincides with the whole argument or discussion. A mere accumulation of meaningless entities, if an isolated proposition were insufficient to give complete meaning, could not do the trick of making the discussion as a whole meaningful. It is true that in art-literature, especially in poetry, the colour and value of a sentence as well as the truth which it tells is contingent upon the surrounding sentences, which force one another into the functional unity of an organism. But this means that if a sentence is ever completely functional and contextual, it is not in argument but in art where it is not the vehicle of a conceptual proposition; but a means to impress by its rhythm, sound, and associations the transformation of ideas, images, and feelings which are inherited from the earlier phases and handed over to the sentences to follow. Thus the operationalists unwittingly give a correct account of sentences as these function in artistic writings.

There is no objection to treating an empirical proposition as a rule when it sets the direction to conceptualization of percepts of a kind. But a rule in this sense is a statement of a condition of actualization of certain tendencies, and as such is either true or false, and not merely efficient or inefficient and calling accordingly for obedience or disobedience. Suppose you taste a plum and find that "This thing is sour". You are implying a rule in the sense of a statement of a condition with a given result: "If one bites the thing one will find it sour." Now the operationalists believe this rule is a command, "Taste it and see that it is sour", and they think that this command is neither true nor false, but an efficient means for testing a flavour. Yet they certainly do not express the original proposition which you know *was* true. Also whether or not the original sentence is a means of organizing a situation, your

Logic and Reality

assent to its truth is a recognition that it is also correct as a *description*. "Taste it and see that it is sour" does not record the fact that you have tasted and have found it sour; it is not even equivalent to "If one bites the thing, one will find it sour", although the latter is a hypothetical proposition which is either true or false. But the hypothetical form is not equivalent to the statement of registering the sensation either, because the former would be true even if you, or anyone else, had never tasted a plum. If, then, an empirical statement exemplified by "The thing is sour" can be called a rule at all, this is not because it can be translated into an equivalent hypothetical proposition or into a command, but because it might not have been expressed at all, or a different conceptualization of the same percept might have been proposed, just as turning the knob of the radio releases only one of the "dispositional" programmes. Once, however, a correct conceptualization has been made, it must be accepted as a true empirical proposition.

The possibility of an alternative set of directions, which seems quite to satisfy calling empirical statements rules, is characteristic of a great many rules, but not of all of them. Outside of empirical statements of fact rules which allow for alternatives are adequately expressed as *commands* which are neither true nor false, although they may be efficient means to some end; but when given in the indicative mood they are "pseudo-propositions" with "truth" by convention.* A familiar illustration is found in

* Some writers refuse to recognize that the drawing of the difference between a proposition as either true or false and a com-

The Problems of Logic

the rules of a game. Take the rule of the game of chess that White makes the first move; it is nothing but a prescription: "Let White make the first move", which is necessary if the game is to continue. To change this command to a description of an actual game, "White makes the first move", one must assume that the attitude of the players keeps them

mand as neither true nor false can be both important and correct by attempting, in protest against the conventionalists, to "reduce" all commands to propositions. For instance, Mr. C. H. Langford, although he does not make clear whether he gives his own or Mr. Black's opinion, writes: "The command, 'close the door', and the prediction, 'you will close the door', present to the hearer precisely the same idea, namely, that of your closing the door. This is shown by the fact that the process of verifying whether the command in such a case is obeyed is identical with that of verifying whether the prediction is true.... To every imperative sentence there corresponds a synonymous indicative sentence." (*Journal of Symb. Log.*, June 1938, p. 93.) But surely, "You will close the door" is, among other things, complemental to a command. It is an assertion that the command "Close the door" will be obeyed, while the command itself not only does not assert this, but, when accompanied with a sanction, betrays fear that without the sanction it would not be obeyed. Thus there seems to be as much reason for identifying "Close the door" with "You will *not* close the door" as for saying that it means "You will close the door". The truth is that a command does not assert anything. Hence a command can be sometimes obeyed and sometimes disobeyed without a change in its logical status, as when some comply and others don't at the shout of "Stick 'm up"; whereas the proposition "All of you will stick 'm up" cannot be sometimes true and sometimes false, but is false if at least one person in the hold-up does not raise his arms. The distinction between the indicative and the imperative moods is a significant fact whose recognition is necessary for the understanding of the difference between a purely postulational method and an axiomatic method as practised by Euclid and defended by Kant.

Logic and Reality

from taking a fancy to let Black start; hence the descriptive form merely conceals the imperative mood by moving it back into the assumption. One might argue that if a player violates a rule of a game, he ceases to play it, and therefore a rule is not only true but a tautology; for example, "White makes the first move" might be taken as an abbreviation of "The game of chess can start only if White makes the first move". Still, there remains a camouflage of a command even in this expounded form, for even if the rules of chess are true by the definition of the game, we know that the game has actually evolved and therefore both its rules and its definition can be changed by convention. A rule is only a command when one follows it because of a decision to do so. By contrast a rule would be more than a command, it would be a genuine proposition or even principle, if one cannot help but follow it in the pursuits of a relevant activity. Thus a rule is either a command or a proposition. In either case a rule can be defined as a statement of a condition under which a certain potentiality is actualized by this rule. The qualification "by this rule", however, is indispensable only when the rule is nothing but a convention so that there are left alternative possibilities of actualization. When Gödel formulates his Rule 1 as: "N shall be an *immediate consequence by Rule 1* of meaningful formulas M_1 and M_2, if and only if there exist formulas A and B such that M_1 is $A \supset B$, M_2 is A and N is B"; he needs the qualifications "by Rule *1*" because entirely different alternative rules could be used in a completely postulational treatment of the object-logic.

The Problems of Logic

The unrestricted treatment of all logical theorems as rules established by convention requires the conviction, which Gödel has proved to be wrong, that it is possible to work out a complete and consistent postulational system of logic. A more moderate conventionalism is satisfied with the assertion that one can disregard *why* the known theorems of logic have been accepted, because, regardless of the actual reasons, one can *also* accept them by convention. Of course, since by convention one means here arbitrary stipulation, one cannot say that logic is established by convention if one chooses to be theorem formulas which he has already known to be true on nonconventional grounds. Nor is conventionalism justified by a reference to luck, which is no less improbable in a procedure of blindly picking out of the list of all kinds of logical expressions all the theorems of the *Principia* than the typing of Shakespeare's plays by Eddington's monkeys. But the conventionalist can argue, without recourse to either luck or antecedent knowledge, that expressions become logical truths automatically if, first, they are formal and, second, stipulated by him as theorems. Let "$A\ B\ C\ B$", which is an arbitrary formal expression, be a theorem. Then it becomes identifiable with any theorem of logic; for example, to identify it with "$\sim p \lor p$", "A" is to be interpreted as "$\sim$", "B" as "p", and "C" as "$\lor$". At first one might think that unrestricted interpretation leads to contradiction. Thus one might point out that if "C" is reinterpreted as ".", while the other letters retain the same interpretation as before, the result is

Logic and Reality

"$\sim p \cdot p$". But since we have agreed to disregard logical truth other than by convention, the expression "$\sim p \cdot p$" *need not mean* now the negation of the principle of non-contradiction; in fact, nothing prevents us from taking the dot in "$\sim p \cdot p$" to mean what is usually meant by "or", in which case the whole expression becomes again identifiable with the principle of the excluded middle. Of course, in adopting an interpretation one must adjust it to the interpretations which have already been given (or are to be given) to the other formal expressions that are stipulated as theorems, but this adjustment also takes place automatically. To illustrate, let us assume, for the sake of argument, that classical logic was right in limiting its fundamental theorems to the three "laws" of identity, non-contradiction, and excluded middle. Suppose the conventionalist likewise stipulated three theorems, (1), (2), and (3). If he symbolizes (1) by "$p \supset p$" and (2) by "$\sim (p \cdot \sim p)$" and identifies them with the principle of identity and the principle of non-contradiction, respectively, he could write, as one usually does, "$p \vee \sim p$" for the principle of the excluded middle. But since he must choose his theorems arbitrarily, he might stipulate as his theorem (3) the expression "$\sim (p \vee \sim p)$". And to prove that his notation is not inconsistent with the principle of the excluded middle, he needs only to point out that *to him* "$\sim (p \vee \sim p)$" means what is usually meant by "$p \vee \sim p$" and that in his use "$\sim ($" has the significance of the identity-function and not of negation. Of course, in this case "$\sim (p \cdot \sim p)$" would not

189

be distinguishable from "$p \, . \sim p$", so that to make these forms stand indifferently for the principle of non-contradiction, one would be forced to determine the meaning of the dot by some such unusual condition as "the affirmation and the negation of a recurrent symbol cannot be both true". This particular treatment of the theorems (1), (2), and (3) is in many ways unsatisfactory, but it illustrates the conventionalist point that by assigning "truth" to a number of originally unmeaning sentences, which comprise different combinations from the same set of symbols, one endows these symbols with meanings that are required by the consistency of the sentences with one another. An elaboration upon this point is found in Dr. W. V. Quine's important article "Truth by Convention".

"A word may, through historical or other accidents, evoke a train of ideas bearing no relevance to the truth or falsehood of its context; in point of *meaning*, however, as distinct from connotation, a word may be said to be determined to whatever extent the truth or falsehood of its context is determined. Such determination of truth or falsehood may be outright, and to that extent the meaning of the word is absolutely determined; or it may be relative to the truth or falsehood of statements containing other words, and to that extent the meaning of the word is determined relatively to those other words. A definition endows a word with complete determinacy of meaning relative to other words. But the alternative is open to us, on introducing a new word, of determining its meaning *absolutely* to whatever

Logic and Reality

extent we like by specifying contexts which are to be true and contexts which are to be false. In fact, we need specify only the former, for falsehood may be regarded as a derivative property depending on the word '∼', in such wise that falsehood of '- - -' means simply truth of '∼ - - -'. Since all contexts of our new word are meaningless to begin with, neither true nor false, we are free to run through the list of such contexts and pick out as true such ones as we like; those selected become true by fiat, by linguistic convention. For those who would question them we have always the same answer, 'You use the word differently.' "*

To this Mr. Quine adds that the arbitrary assignment of truth need not be restricted by consideration of consistency. For suppose "truth" is assigned to both '- - -' and '∼ - - -'. No inconsistency will result, "We sin only against the established usage of '∼' as a denial sign. Under the latter usage '- - -' and '∼ - - -' are not both true; in taking them both by convention as true we merely endow the sign '∼', roughly speaking, with a meaning other than denial."†

* Cf. *Essays for Whitehead*, Longmans, Green & Co., 1936, p. 104.

† Ibid., p. 112. According to Dr. Quine the method of assigning "truth" to theorems taken one by one must give way to the ordinary postulational procedure, because the listing of all logical theorems whose number is infinite is impossible. But it seems to me that the conventionalist could be satisfied even if his claim were restricted to the finite (although very large) list of all theorems of logic that have been actually formulated at some time or other.

In the main Dr. Quine and I take similar attitudes towards con-

The Problems of Logic

The appraisal of this theory is made easier by explaining why the procedure of arbitrary assignment of "truth", which determines the meanings of terms, cannot be extended from purely logical formula to empirical statements. Suppose we attempt to establish the meaning of the word "W" by various assignments of "truth" in the list of five empirical statements:

(1) W can bark;
(2) W can swim;
(3) W has at least two legs;
(4) W can speak English;
(5) W has four legs.

I assume that words other than "W" in this list have been previously defined in a general agreement with their use in English. Now let us assign T (i.e. truth by convention) to (1); we might think that "W" is another word for "dog", but then seals also bark and even if we assign T to (2) we cannot decide between the two meanings. The assignment of T to (3) rules out the seal, but if we add (4) as "true", nothing remains but to identify "W" with an English clown. The real difficulty, however, appears only when we accept as "true" all five statements. To the reader's protest that they deprive "W" of meaning, the conventionalist can only answer that the meaning of "W" is given by its use in the context of the above five statements. But he has no

ventionalism, but, for reasons given in the text, I disagree with his assertion that *if* logic can be established by convention, so can empirical truth.

Logic and Reality

answer when it is further pointed out that nothing in experience corresponds to "W" thus used and that therefore, *as empirical statements*, the five sentences in which "W" occurs are meaningless. Since observation and not convention is the source of the truth of an empirical statement, empirical terms must have *denotation* and no contextual definition can either conflict with or disregard their denotative meanings. If logical theorems, unlike empirical truth, can be established by convention, it is because they have no external standards to conform to and because their abstract terms, although contextually significant, have no denotation.

To take an opposite stand, to insist that logical convention no less than empirical truth has reference to an external situation, one could try to argue as follows.* The theorems of logic as we actually know them have not been established by convention, even if they could be so established; and this means that they have to be taken into consideration, indeed have to be used as standards to guide the construction of a logic by convention. A set of "logical truths by convention" must be isomorphous with the set of logical principles known antecedently and on independent grounds; for if they are not isomorphous, if there is no notational dictionary to translate one set into the other, then there is no reason to call the conventional set "logic", even in quotations marks, or even to take it as anything but strings of figures which can be called "true" only by depriving the word "truth" of any definite

* Please see page 196.

meaning. Take again "the laws of thought" established by treating as theorems three sets of marks on paper: (1) $p \supset p$; (2) $\sim (p \, . \sim p)$; and (3) $p \lor \sim p$. To invest these marks with distinctions of significance, with distinctive structures that allow for identification of (1) with the law of identity, of (2) with the law of non-contradiction, and of (3) with the law of the excluded middle, the conventionalist must have an antecedent knowledge of the structures of these laws on some independent grounds. Without such knowledge he not only would not know what meanings to give to the individual marks, and therefore what to mean by each of the three formulas, but he could not even decide whether or not (1), (2), and (3) are three different transcriptions of the same truth by convention, i.e. whether or not they are different theorems. In a sense, as the truth-table shows, the three laws of thought are tautologies and therefore they do say the same thing, but neither their identity of informative value nor their difference in conceptual articulation can be understood by merely inspecting three different strings of marks on paper.

But it is obvious that the force of this argument depends on the assumption that just as in the case of empirical truth, logical theorems by convention must be established in conformity with antecedently known principles such as "the laws of thought". I believe that this assumption is incorrect for nearly all theorems, and my evidence is the existence of alternative systems of logic. Thus one need not interpret formula (3) as "the law of the excluded

Logic and Reality

middle", since in a three-valued logic this "law" is not a theorem. The possibility of discarding a theorem by adopting a different logic proves that the theorem has no external antecedent standard to be adjusted to; at the same time this possibility proves that the theorem is not an irreplaceable principle but a mere rule or convention that is in use as long as someone wishes to play the game. On the other hand, logic is not simply a game. If it were, alternative logics would differ from one another not less than chess differs from tennis; we know that this is not so, since we classify them all under the same name of *logic*. There must be principles, however few, which are common to all alternative systems and which no system can omit without ceasing to be logic. As explained before, at least the principles of non-contradiction and of logical significance are examples of such necessary non-conventional truth.

The treatment of logical theorems as being, with a few exceptions, mere rules has, among other consequences, an unfavourable effect on the postulationalist opposition between metalogic and object-logic. For the rules of procedure are concerned with the transformation of formulas of the object-logic, and, therefore, being about the object-logic, they belong to metalogic. So long as the theorems are contrasted with these rules and treated as formulas, the object-logic remains a sizeable body. But as soon as the theorems themselves become rules they must be transferred to metalogic, since now their difference from the rules of procedure is

The Problems of Logic

primarily notational: while the rules of inference are given in ordinary language, the theorems are formulated in symbols. And it would seem that with the annexation of theorems by metalogic, nothing is left for the object-logic but to disappear.* On the other hand, if logic by convention has been a set-back to the intuitionalist, he still has his intuitive justification of the few basic principles of logic such as the principle of non-contradiction. Furthermore, given the rules by convention, their application in the actual transformation of formulas into one another still requires intuition in the act of conceptual discernment of the structure of a formula.

* The usual notation suggests that logical theorems are not propositions. Thus one writes, for the principle of the excluded middle, "$p \lor \sim p$" rather than "$(p) . (p \lor \sim p)$", and the first expression is a propositional function. This gives a further suggestion that a propositional function is a technical equivalent of a rule. Thus "$\frac{4}{2} = x$" can be read "Divide 4 by 2"; "fx" may be interpreted as a *prescription* to obtain a proposition by assigning the property f to any individual, and so on. According to this view, the relation between a propositional function and a corresponding proposition is a relation between a rule and a performance which either conforms with or violates the rule.

Reference to page 193.]

* If empirical truth had alternatives, the animal "W" (as described by the five empirical statements in the text) might exist in some unsuspected realm of fact. As it is, alternatives to empirical truth are found in fiction only, and even there the basic constitution of reality must be assumed without change. Thus while novels describe imaginary men and women, the empirical terms "man" and "woman" are used in the description in the ordinary sense. In

Logic and Reality

abstract logic, on the other hand, there are alternative systems of form, and even such fundamental logical terms as "proposition" have one meaning in a two-valued system and another in a many-valued system.

Yet Dr. Quine has raised an objection: " . . . uninterpretability of 'W' could have been obtained within the medium of logical expressions by the same method; if e.g. we suppose 'V', 'A', and 'C' interpreted in advance, then there is no possible interpretation of 'W' fulfilling the pair of conditions:

$$VCW \quad , \quad WCA".$$

But the conventionalist would reject this condition, not because "W" is meaningless, but because of the conjunction "$(\exists W).[CVCW).(WCA)]$" which contradicts the already accepted theorem "$(W).[\sim(VCW)V\sim(WCV)]$," where "$W$" stands for *any* class. If, however, the theorem is not accepted, the conventionalist can treat "W" as a *special* term, perhaps as a function of the sign "C" which is equal to "V" when "W" occurs on the right of "C" and to "A" when it is on the left. No such tricky treatment can be given to an empirical "W" since then it is used to designate an actual object and not as a function of signs.

Chapter VI

THE EXISTENCE OF PROPOSITIONS

§ 1. Introduction

A favourite point with those who insist on the separation of logic and metalogic is that only by means of such a separation can one distinguish between using and talking about symbols; and to fall in line with this, one must take "true" and "false", as referring to propositions in the nth language, to be themselves words in the $(n + 1)$th language. Unfortunately the prescribed distinction between using and talking about symbols breaks down as soon as qualifications of significance are introduced into logic. For example, consider the set of symbols which is usually interpreted as the calculus of unanalysed propositions. Of course, there are many statements about these symbols, such as considerations of consistency, which are outside the calculus; I should say that they belong to the theory of the calculus; nevertheless, within the symbolic complexes of the calculus itself one can still distinguish between symbols which are interpreted as unanalysed propositions and symbols which are about the former. Thus in "$p \supset q$" the horseshoe is about the proposition-symbols p and q, it symbolizes the implication of q by p. In particular note that one cannot remove the qualification of falsehood outside the symbolic complexes of the calculus, for when

The Existence of Propositions

"$\sim p$" is interpreted in the usual manner, it stands for the expression "It is false that p".

If we brand the above difficulty as specious, this is because we prefer to treat symbolic formulas as "shorthand" for technical statements which belong to the theory of logic; for instance, we take "$p \supset q$" to be an abbreviation of "A certain proposition implies another" or, perhaps, of "The truth of one proposition implies the truth of another". In our treatment the horseshoe is not about the symbols p and q, but all three symbols co-operate in the function of abbreviating the *description* of a certain relationship among actual propositions; all three of them are *about* complexes of actual discourse. Accordingly, we should use the symbols p, q, etc., at least when these occur in the context of truth-functions, not as proposition-variables, but, rather, as ambiguous *descriptions* of propositions. For example, the truth-function "$\sim p$" is to be interpreted not as "It is false that p", where p designates any proposition, but as "The proposition expressed by a sentence which is symbolized by 'p' is false". One might find such an interpretation to be too cumbersome, especially when it is extended from unanalysed propositions to statements of actual discourse. And, of course, to require that a simple sentence like "It is false that there are green cats" be replaced by the involved expression "The proposition expressed by the sentence 'There are green cats' is false" is to ask for an awkward complication. But however undesirable the complications, the disadvantages seem to be outweighed by what we gain from the proposed interpretation. First, it allows us to do justice to the fact that the constituents of truth-functions (other than conjunctions) are not meant to be asserted; this fact remains unintelligible as long as the constituents are taken to be propositions which claim truth. Thus in "$p \supset q$" the constituents on either side of the horseshoe are merely supposed without being asserted; hence the reading "If p were true, then q would be true" is more adequate than the usual reading "If p is true, then q is true". But the phrase "If p *were* true" would be meaningless if p were a designation of a self-assertive proposition and therefore equivalent to "p is true". To avoid any ambiguity and to shift assertion from the constituents to where it belongs, to the implication as whole, one should read the latter as "The (truth of the) proposition expressed by the sentence 'p' implies the (truth of the) proposition expressed by the sentence 'q'", i.e. as an expression the constituents of which are descriptive phrases. Second, the use of descriptions instead of designations would be welcome to writers who see no meaning in self-contradiction and therefore find it difficult to account for the formula "$p \,.\, \sim p$", because it gives the needed account by letting "$p \,.\, \sim p$" mean:

"The propositions expressed by the sentences 'p' and '$\sim p$' are both true."

This expresses a false but significant proposition, and when we say that it is false, we see that the principle of non-contradiction "$\sim (p \,.\, \sim p)$" is read

The Existence of Propositions

"The proposition expressed by the sentence '$p . \sim p$' is false."*

Third, the claim to truth of a proposition p entails the statement that this proposition is true, but the original proposition cannot be identical with the entailed statement, for if it were, it would be incomplete because of the infinite regress from "p" to "p is true", "It is true that p is true", and so on. But the difference between "p" and "p is true" would be something intangible, unless the same symbol "p", which in isolation designates a proposition, stands in combination with "true" for the descriptive phrase "the proposition expressed by the sentence 'p'".† If the reader is ready to agree with these remarks he must yet realize one thing: They all presuppose the distinction between a sentence and a proposition, and, therefore, the existence of propositions. Yet many writers have questioned the existence of propositions, primarily on the ground that, unlike sentences, propositions are not observ-

* Note that the phrase "The proposition expressed by the sentence '$p . \sim p$' . . ." does not imply the existence of a self-contradictory proposition unless one falls back upon the usual interpretation of '$p . \sim p$'. Cf. my article "The Calculus of propositions and self-contradiction", *The Philosophical Review*, May 1939.

† Against treating the constituents of truth-functions as descriptions rather than propositions one might argue that this deprives propositions of the possibility of entering into logical relations with one another. A possible answer to this objection is that the relations of propositions are grasped by logical intuition in a more direct way than the use of logical constants can ever express. Intuition reveals the fact that falsehood is not a part of truth, and it is this fact which finds indirect expression in the formula "$p \supset q$".

able entities. And such doubts have led to attempts at explaining situations which might appear to require the presence of propositions in terms which actually dispense with the latter. Of these attempts the latest, I believe, is found in C. D. Broad's *Examination of McTaggart's Philosophy*.*

Broad's thesis is that any statement can be analysed exclusively in terms of facts and sentences. I agree with Broad so far as true statements are in question, because, as explained in § 3 of Chapter V, a true proposition is identical with a fact taken in the sense of a conceptualized registration or analysis of an event. One might, of course, deny the existence of propositions even in this sense, which would amount to the opinion that the word "fact" must be used in its other sense only, as a designation of an event or a process of actuality. But this view is obviously incorrect; to controvert it one can use the evidence of such *facts* as *Plato lived before Kant*, which does not designate any particular event or process. However, there is no need to argue the point here, because there is no reason to think that Broad himself would restrict the meaning of the word "fact" to that of "event".† Hence I should not object to Broad at all, if it were not for the existence of *false* propositions. But let us see, first, how he tries to explain them away by using in his account nothing

* Cf. Vol. I, Cambridge University Press 1933, ch. iv.

† Thus in referring to one's knowledge of the fact that the other side of this paper must have some colour or other, Broad gives an example of a fact about an event which cannot be identified with the event itself.

The Existence of Propositions

but sentences and facts. Let the statement be "The other side of this sheet is blue", which the reader will find, by turning this page, to be false; but suppose I accept the statement without turning the page to see if the back be blue. According to Broad's analysis my mistaken belief involves several *facts* of knowledge, viz.:

> "(i) I know that there is another side of the paper. (ii) I know that this other side must have some colour or other, if white and black be counted as colours. (iii) I know, with regard to blue, green, yellow, red, white, and black, that they are determinates which fall under the determinable of colour. . . ."

In (i), (ii), and (iii) there is no need for propositions because they are concerned with *direct* knowledge of facts. My mistaken belief about the other side of the paper contains also a thought of blue which is a psychological fact or event. Finally, this belief *associates* my knowledge as described in (i), (ii), and (iii), by means of a special relation which Broad calls the relation of "being inserted", with my thought of blue. The association is another psychological fact, and when it takes place I use the sentence "The other side of this sheet of paper is blue" in its proper sense.

But if Broad is right and nothing except facts and knowledge of facts is involved in a false belief, its falsehood is a mystery. Broad tries to explain: "My belief is false if and only if the thought which stands to my states of knowing in the relation of being inserted is the thought of one of the other determinate colours" than the colour which in fact characterizes the other side of the paper, e.g. it is the thought of blue provided the other side of the paper is white. Of course, Broad can define "falsehood" in any way he pleases, but his definition is certainly arbitrary unless the relation of being inserted is not merely an innocent psychological association of a thought of some determinate characteristic with one's state of knowledge but an assertion of the objective validity of such an association, i.e. a claim to its truth. There is nothing false in one's image or thought of "the other side of the paper as being blue"; falsehood arises only when the image or the thought of "the other side of the paper as being blue" is taken to be not merely an image or a thought but a representation of a fact. But if the relation of being inserted is used to represent a fact, it becomes in this use just another name for the *proposition* that the other side of the paper is blue. It is possible that Broad would give a different interpretation to his relation of being inserted, but it is difficult to see how any interpretation which is not an assumption that a proposition is an object of a false belief or judgment could do justice to the existence of falsehood.*

* In a discussion in *Mind* (1931) Mr. Ryle and Mr. Richard Robinson have both tried to explain falsehood without the aid of false propositions. But Mr. Robinson's attempt has been refuted by Mr. Ryle. As to Mr. Ryle himself, his account of falsehood is in terms of a would-be statement of fact if there were such; in his own words, "if so and so was the case, the statement *would* state the fact". Let us take the false statement "The earth is flat". It would seem to be Mr. Ryle's intention to interpret it thus: "If the earth

The Existence of Propositions

Where Broad has failed, others may succeed; hence no defence of propositions can be entirely satisfactory unless some positive evidence for their existence is produced. Granted that propositions, unlike sentences, are not observable, one can still argue that propositions exist as indispensable conditions of discourse, which is embodied in sentences. Let us accept as a definition of the proposition that it is the *meaning or interpretation of an indicative sentence*; we then can point out that transition from a spoken to a written sentence or translation from one language to another is conditioned by the fact that though there is a change in the sentences, their meaning, which is a proposition, remains the same, and this requires, of course, the existence of propositions as distinct from sentences. The sceptics might reply that "invariance of meaning throughout changing sentences" is merely a phrase behind which there is nothing but a conventional correlation of spoken and written sentences as well as of sentences which belong to different languages. But there are at least two more points in favour of propositions: they are needed as bearers of truth-value and as communicable units in discourse.

§ 2. Propositions as Objects of Truth-value

The distinction between a sentence and a propo-

were flat, then the statement to that effect would state a fact." But this interpretation is a tautology and not a falsehood. Also, the formulation of its condition presupposes the existence of the false proposition in question.

The Problems of Logic

sition is a contrast between a merely verbal expression and a conceptual expression. A proposition is an expression because it bestows articulate form on our knowledge of things; it is conceptual because this articulation is a conceptualization of what otherwise would be an undifferentiated tendency. The adequacy of conceptual articulation is the meaning of "truth", and therefore nothing but a proposition can be true or false. For example, a sentence in abstraction from its conceptual meaning is, as Whitehead puts it, "a series of squeaks", which merely *is* or takes place as any other natural process that one cannot significantly tag with a truth-qualification.* Likewise a judgment as a mental act is an event of nature and not an object of truth-value; if we call a judgment correct or incorrect, we do it by courtesy, i.e. with reference to the truth of a proposition which the judgment either accepts or rejects. The derivative nature of the correctness of a judgment must be recognized if we observe that while we change our mind and accept a proposition which we used to reject, we are aware that the change of judgment has not affected the truth of the proposition. Thus it has always been false that "The earth is flat", even though only five centuries ago people took it to be true.

Some writers refer to Whitehead in support of the view that while propositions exist, their existence does not require association with truth-value. But Whitehead, on the contrary, has emphatically

* Cf. *Process and Reality*, Cambridge University Press, 1929, p. 374.

The Existence of Propositions

asserted that "A proposition must be true or false".* What Whitehead objects to is the exclusive association of propositions with judgments, and not their association with truth-values: "The conception of propositions as merely material for judgments is fatal to any understanding of their rôle in the universe."† But in attributing this conception to logicians Whitehead is just as guilty of misinterpretation as some logicians are guilty of misinterpreting him. For, using W. E. Johnson's terminology, logicians admit the existence of epistemic attitudes towards a proposition other than the attitude of judging. A proposition can be entertained, or doubted, or assumed, or even figure as a "lure for feeling"; the only restriction upon the range of epistemic attitudes being their relevance to the consideration of truth; and the nature of this restriction is itself further evidence for the association of propositions with truth-values. But to decide the matter with even more conclusive evidence, observe that dissociation from truth-value would make propositions indistinguishable from propositional functions which would leave no explanation for truth and falsehood since these cannot arise through the act of judgment, at least not when the latter is defined as an appraisal of a proposition with regard to its truth or falsehood.

The association with truth or falsehood is, of course, a different thing from the claim to truth, and Whitehead, for one, asserts that "its own truth, or

* Cf. *Process and Reality*, Cambridge University Press, 1929, p. 363. Cf. also p. 264 and p. 365. † Ibid., p. 363.

its own falsity, is no business of a proposition."*
Yet elsewhere Whitehead admits that "the form of words in which propositions are framed also includes an incitement to the origination of an affirmative judgment feeling".† Also he uses the expression "the proposition proposes as a physical fact".‡ It seems to me that the embodiment of a proposition in the form of words which incite affirmation would be unintelligible unless one wanted to give verbal expression to the claim to truth, and that to propose something as a fact is the same thing as to claim truth. To my mind the claim to truth is indispensable to a proposition because without it the proposition could not be false, just as without a pretension to speak truthfully one would not be a liar. Also, one cannot judge a proposition unless one agrees or disagrees with it, but except for the claim to truth there is nothing in a proposition which calls for agreement or disagreement. Finally, only the claim to truth, called by W. E. Johnson "the assertive tie", distinguishes a proposition from the corresponding descriptive phrase which already contains "the characterizing tie":

> "The blending of the assertive with the characterizing tie is expressed in language by the transition from the participal, subordinate, or relative clause, to the finite or declaratory form of the principal verb. Thus in passing from 'a

---

* Cf. *Process and Reality*, Cambridge University Press, 1929, p. 365.
† Ibid., p. 367.   ‡ Ibid., p. 371.

The Existence of Propositions

child fearing a dog' to 'a child fears a dog', the characterizing tie joins the same elements, in the same way, in both cases, but is, in the latter, blended with the assertive tie."*

An objection is often raised to the effect that propositions, being inanimate, can neither propose nor claim nor do anything; and this is, of course, true if propositions are taken in abstraction from actual thinking. But I hold such an abstraction illegitimate, because I believe that the objective nature of a proposition, which is its independence of a particular thought of some particular person, does not mean that a proposition can exist outside of some thought or other. To say that a proposition claims truth is really to say, first, that the thought of a proposition is an assertion and, second, that while the assertive element is dissociated from thought as "this particular act", it can be identified with the significance of the proposition as such because the same import of assertion would be given by any particular thought at all and because a judgment can disown an assertion which the thought of the proposition presents.† As to the statement that propositions must exist in the medium of thought,

* W. E. Johnson, *Logic*, Cambridge University Press, vol. i, p. 12.

† Thinking is dramatic: one can argue with oneself and one also can understand, i.e. live through the assertions of others, without accepting them or even while rejecting them. The thought of a proposition in abstraction from one's epistemic attitude towards it is similar to his understanding of another person's assertion; it requires a reproduction of the assertive import in thought without giving a sanction to it.

The Problems of Logic

this is a form of conceptualism and, of course, a metaphysical theory, but, once the existence of propositions is admitted, conceptualism is best because it involves a minimum of metaphysical assumption; the alternative doctrine that propositions dwell in the realm of subsistence even when no one thinks of them is certainly much more metaphysical.*

§ 3. Perceptual Judgments

Perceptual judgments are not acts of accepting or rejecting propositions because they are directly concerned with the characterization of presentations, i.e. of particulars or sense-data or memory-images; hence the question whether they, like propositions, are really objects of truth-value, requires special consideration. One complication of this question is the fact that many perceptual judgments are not proper objects of logical discussion, because no one with the exception of the person who made a judgment can be sure that he understood it. The judgment of perception "This is white" may not mean the same thing to the reader as to the writer, unless I add to the judgment the explanation that I have in mind this sheet of paper. Prior to my explanation the reader would have to be content with an interpretation of my judgment, which is a proposition with

---

* Some logicians argue that because it is possible to think of one and the same proposition at different times, it has not disappeared in the interim. But to my mind the idea of recurring propositions is more intelligible than the idea of a proposition which persists outside thought in some mysterious field of reality.

The Existence of Propositions

a weaker import than the judgment, viz. with the singular proposition "The thing (that the writer means) is white". Yet some perceptual judgments can be communicated to the reader without loss of import. For example, if instead of "This is white" I write "This sheet is white", I succeed in communicating my meaning in the sense that any reader can check my judgment by his own.* But let us, for the sake of argument, disregard the question of communicability and concentrate on the association of the truth-values with the simplest kind of perceptual judgments which I have illustrated, using at random this sheet of paper, by my judgment "This is white". Some logicians call such a simple perceptual judgment "infallible" or "incorrigible" meaning that "true" but not "false" can be properly applied to it.† Others, however, go even further and take "This is white" to be a rule of language, and not a true or false statement. I shall first criticize the dissociation of truth-value from perceptual judgments in its radical form, as one finds it in Mr. Friedrich Waismann's contribution to the symposium on "The Relevance of Psychology to Logic",

* If one takes for granted that the words "sheet" and "white" have the same meaning to me and to the reader, his judgment "This sheet is white" is either a duplicate or has the same function as mine; it is an exact duplicate if both of us use "this" to designate the same particular; it has the same function if each of us is concerned with his own private sense-datum or memory-image.

† Only the simplest perceptual judgments like "This is white" are incorrigible, because a slightly more complicated assertion "This sheet is white" could be false if one would make it while seeing it in the mirror and unaware of the fact that he sees merely a reflection.

The Problems of Logic

but my later criticism will also be applicable to the more moderate view which allows for true judgments of perception.*

According to Mr. Waismann in judging that "This is white" or, more simply, in calling out "White" whenever one perceives the appearance of a white patch, one merely practises a correct use of the word "White", i.e. a use in accordance with English. If one should call "black" instead, this would mean no falsehood but a misuse of English, i.e. either a slip of the tongue or a misunderstanding of the word. There is no falsehood because the rules of good English do not allow for calling white "black", and therefore, if one does, one ceases to speak English; his utterance "This is black" is pseudo-English rather than false; it is "a falsely formed proposition, but not a false proposition". Mr. Waismann sums up as follows:

> "What is the case in this example holds, I think, of every description of immediate experience. If I describe a pain, a sound, or any other experience, the only question that can be raised is whether or not I use the words correctly in accordance with the rules of language; but not whether my utterance is true or false. What, then, is the nature of the utterance? It is not a proposition, if we understand by a proposition something which can be true or false. . . . It corresponds to what Schlick has called a '*Konstatierung*'. . . . I cannot doubt

* *Proceedings of Aristotelian Society*, Supplementary Volume XVII, 1938, p. 54.

The Existence of Propositions

a *Konstatierung*, not because I am so sure of it that I cannot mistrust it, but because to doubt it doesn't make sense."*

Mr. Waismann proceeds to contrast a perceptual judgment or a *Konstatierung*, in which perceptual experience comes first and the word is uttered afterwards, with a genuine proposition illustrated by one's guess that the page on the other side of this sheet will be found to be white; and he explains that in the genuine proposition the word "white" is used in anticipation of perception, which allows, according to the rules of language, for the alternative of a correct or of an incorrect guess, i.e. for truth and falsity. To be capable of alternative truth-values a proposition must anticipate and therefore be about the future.

Mr. Waismann's explanation must appear extremely questionable to any reader of *Scientific Thought* who remembers and appreciates C. D. Broad's argument that a statement about the future, being at the moment when it is made not yet true or false, is not a proposition. But even more detrimental to Mr. Waismann's view is the recognition of the fact that verification, which Mr. Waismann as a logical positivist must identify with the proposition itself, is based on a *Konstatierung* or judgment of perception. Take again the guess that the page on the other side of this sheet is white; to verify it I must turn this page and confront my guess with

* *Proceedings of Aristotelian Society*, Supplementary Volume XVII, 1938, p. 60.

The Problems of Logic

a statement which is either "What I have guessed is so" or "What I have guessed is not so". But verification, i.e. the statement "What I have guessed is so", is obviously dependent on the *Konstatierung* "This is white". Since, however, to Mr. Waismann a *Konstatierung* is merely a correct use of words, it would seem that he is forced to hold the absurdity that verification of statements of fact is a matter of linguistics.

The idea of the correct use of language is itself far from being clear. As I understand Mr. Waismann, he believes that those who speak or write in accordance with the rules of language need not be consciously aware of the rules in use.* This belief is probably true, but it raises a metaphysical problem concerning the status of a rule which holds even if it is not explicitly stated and deliberately adhered to; and the problem is certainly real, at least when it comes to specific rules dealing with the use of a particular word such as "white", for these rules are not listed in the books of grammar and syntax. Suppose we ask Mr. Waismann to state the rule of how to use the word "white"; he might suggest the following formulation: "Apply the word 'white' to any perception which is similar to your perception of the colour of this page", but this suggestion gives

---

* Ibid., p. 67. Mr. Waismann concedes to Russell that the psychological association between a word and its meaning may be a causal connection, but thinks that logically this is immaterial, because "the calculus proceeds no matter what are the causes which determine its separate steps". One observes the rules of the calculus if one acts as if one deliberately applied the rules, even though in fact the act is automatic or mechanically determined.

The Existence of Propositions

too narrow an interpretation of the rule in question, for the understanding of this rule must not be confined to the readers of this book. A rule of language, however specific, must be communicable to anyone speaking the language. Thus the difficulty of restricted communicability which we have tried to disregard while discussing the identification of perceptual judgments with rules of language is forced back upon us as an outcome of this very discussion. Now let us point out one aspect of this difficulty in criticism of Mr. Waismann as well as of those who take perceptual judgments to be infallibly true.

One reason why a judgment of perception is not transferable is that the datum designated by the word "this" is not something static and determinate, but a process undergoing continuous modifications during the act of passing the judgment. As I look at this page in the electric light and frame the judgment "This is white", I begin to doubt whether "it" is not rather pale yellow. Let no one tell me that the "this" of the judgment is a different datum from the "it" of the doubt to follow. I did not have the experience of numerically distinct data, I have referred to the same thing although at different stages of its perceptual specification. And when I recognize this, I realize that the initial stage was insufficient to warrant my characterization of the datum as being white, and that therefore the judgment of perception "This is white" was false. To give another illustration, it is often said that one cannot err when one finds himself in pain; but the statement is ambiguous. Of course, when one knows that he is in pain, he cannot deny it; yet one may not know it for sure while living through an intermediate phase of physical unrest which is a fringe of undifferentiated experience between pain and pleasure. A perceptual judgment can be false, because before the maximum specificity of perception is reached it is not a unified conception but rather thought in the making which allows for indefinite expansion in a transaction with the datum whereby the latter assumes a higher degree of determination.

§ 4. THE UNIT OF THOUGHT

A search for the communicable units of thought begins with the logic of terms, moves towards the logic of judgments, and is forced to discard judgments for propositions. In following this course of the transformation of the unit of logic I shall outline the main reasons for its particular order without trying to be faithful to the details of history. I shall use the word "statement" as a neutral designation for either a sentence or a proposition or a judgment and "term" for any element of a statement which is not itself a statement.

The *logic of terms* is identifiable with aristotelean tradition; it is a substantival theory of terms, i.e. it takes terms to be apprehended directly or by acquaintance and therefore to be independent of context. This logic has many varieties conditioned by different explanations of the nature of terms. One of the least sophisticated explanations, the image-theory of terms, confuses terms with images; when

The Existence of Propositions

the objection is raised that images are private possessions of individual minds and cannot function as communicable entities, the defenders of the image-theory often reply by talking about "composite-images" without realizing that composition out of the original data is also a subjective procedure, the results of which vary from one person to another. The rejection of the image-theory of terms leaves logicians still divided (with regard to the status of terms) among the camps of realism, conceptualism, and nominalism, but whatever their metaphysical position, as long as they agree that the meaning of term is independent of the context of statements they must construe a statement to be the result of mechanical association or dissociation of terms, viz. as an outcome of *predication* whereby one term, the predicate, is assigned to or denied of the other term, the subject. Thus the logic of terms finds a natural expression in the subject-predicate logic; and this logic continues to satisfy while science remains on the primitive level of characterizing and classifying empirical data, since predication covers both the relation of characterization (or class-membership) and of class-inclusion. Nevertheless, as the emphasis is shifted from the data to their relations, transition to the *logic of judgment*, where judgment is the unit of predication, becomes inevitable.*

---

* Historically this transition was conditioned by Porphyry's interpretation of Aristotle's doctrine of categories. To introduce the issue involved in this interpretation let us ask the question whether a term has logical significance in its own right or must acquire it through predication. Can one think of a "man" without thinking

The Problems of Logic

When judgment is taken as the unit of thought, this means that it cannot be broken into constituent-terms without altering the meaning which they have in context. Terms cease to be regarded as fixed meanings: it is believed that an idea changes when transferred from one context of thought into another, and that outside the organic unity of context ideas die out. The thesis of this logic is that judgment is the minimum context because it is a single organic act of thought which modifies the terms involved by forcing them into a fusion where they interpenetrate. The main weakness of the logic of judgment is that its units are neither objective nor communicable; a judgment as an act of thought is a mental event which, like any other event, is unique and non-transferable; there is no way of telling whether predication as an act in one mind modifies the terms in the same way as it would in another mind. It follows that as a context judgment is unstable; to stabilize it, i.e. to prove that it can be invariant at least through recurrence of similar ideas in the minds of thinkers, one must check it against other judgments, which requires an extension of the context; and this procedure of extension has no limit

of a "substance", or are these thoughts connected because of the judgment "A man is a substance"? This question corresponds to the issue of logical priority between Aristotle's categories and predicables (Cf. Topics, 1, 9). Porphyry decided in favour of the predicables, and his decision must have influenced the transition from the logic of terms to the logic of judgments in spite of the counter-influence of such men as William of Occam. (Cf. W. D. Ross, *Aristotle*, second edition, London, 1930, p. 57, and E. A. Moody, *The Logic of William Ockham*, Sheed & Ward, N.Y., 1935.)

The Existence of Propositions

short of the whole field of discourse.* Yet the whole discourse must be built up discursively, step by step, and since each successive step is a single judgment, there appears to be a vicious circle; while the whole cannot be grasped without the understanding of its constituents, the meaning of the constituents is derived from the meaning of the whole.

The *logic of propositions* solves the difficulty of the logic of judgments without falling back upon the doctrine of atomic terms. A proposition is a context and allows its subordinate terms only a contextual significance; at the same time it is a unit-context because it is a complete meaning, not in the sense of a complete truth, but in the sense of being completely true. A proposition has no need for a larger context to stabilize its meaning, because by definition it is the objective element of a judgment and therefore does not suffer from the subjectivity of the latter. A thought has two major aspects: there is the act of thinking and there is its content or concern. Acts of thinking, such as judgments, are subjective, but their concern, a proposition, is not; for the same proposition can be thought of in many acts, either at different times by the same mind, or at the same time through communication. Its invariance, and independence of particular acts of thought or judgment, not only enable the proposition to serve as a communicable and objective unit, but likewise to

* This explains why the logic of judgments is intimately connected with absolute idealism which discredits any knowledge short of the knowledge of the absolute. (Cf. C. R. Morris, *Idealistic Logic*, London, Macmillan, 1933.)

The Problems of Logic

take a form which differs from the structure of a mental act. While "predication" may be the natural form of a judgment, the proposition can embody relations of other kinds as well, and therefore is a proper unit not only for classificatory science but for any field of discourse, including mathematics as the science of orders and relationships. Finally, when logic is taken in extension, its communicable and objective units must be defined by consideration of truth-values. As already mentioned judgment does not endow the proposition which is judged with objective truth or falsehood, and therefore cannot function as the unit of thought. It is obvious that a term, even more than a judgment, is unfit to be a unit of truth-value.*

---

* The two-valued algebra endows a term with a truth-value by postulating that "$a = (a = 1)$", where "a" is a term and "1" stands for "truth". But this postulate forces upon the algebra a propositional interpretation of terms (not because "1" must be interpreted as "truth", but because "$=$" is interpreted as "equal to"), and therefore the units of the calculus are propositions and not terms. The disadvantage of this procedure (as compared with the calculus of unanalysed propositions) is well known: it leads to a confusion between an element "a" and a statement about this element "$a = 1$".

Given a proposition "p", a distinction must be made between "p" and "$p = 1$" as well as between "$p = 1$" and "$\vdash p$". The symbol "$\vdash$" indicates the necessity of asserting the formula which follows it and, therefore, can be taken, subjectively, as the writer's rule for making a judgment of assertion or else, objectively, as an index to a logical principle or theorem. In any case it belongs to the theory of logic and cannot be contradicted within the calculus. On the other hand, "$p = 1$" is within the calculus (even though it is about "p") and may be false; it expresses, explicitly, as a statement

The Existence of Propositions

Many contemporary writers prefer the *logic of sentences* to the logic of propositions, but from the point of view of its fitness to function as an objective and communicable unit a sentence is decidedly inferior to a proposition. To illustrate, let us take again the sentence "This is white". As a *perceptual* experience of the reader it is his private event which is not communicable to anyone else. As a physical process which goes on at the 6th line from the top of this page it can be described by a physicist, but is beyond the cognizance of a layman; in any event it is not serviceable as a means of communication because it cannot be observed by either a physicist or a layman. There are additional difficulties if, instead of taking the sentence to be the particular *instance* as it appears on the 6th line of this page, one defines the sentence as the *class* of similar instances, i.e. the class whose members are: "This is white", "This is white", "This is white", etc., or as the *pattern* after which these instances are shaped. But even leaving aside such complications, one must admit that unless it is a series of words which is unified by meaning, i.e. unless its unity is derivative from and secondary to the unity of a proposition, the sentence is no more intrinsically a unit than the letters which form its constituent-words or than

---

the claim to truth which "p" has implicitly, as a mode of significance. I cannot be positive but I believe that Professor B. A. Bernstein's interesting criticism of the *Principia* is weakened by his identification of "$p = 1$" with "$\vdash p$" and by a failure to recognize that a proposition symbolized by "p", although distinct from "$p = 1$", entails the latter.

these words themselves. To perception, at least, a single letter or a symbol stands out as a unit much more conspicuously than a sentence, especially when the latter is spread over a number of lines; and therefore it is not surprising that in the latest development of the calculus of sentences, in the combinatory logic of Schönfinkel and Curry, a disruption of a sentence into its constituent-symbols as the basic units of computation has actually taken place. But such a disruption is obviously a step back to the *logic of terms* treated nominalistically, and this regress closes the cycle of transformation of the logical unit.

INDEX

Abstract system, 12, 154
Ackerman, 23, 94 f.
Adjective, 137–42
Alternative logic, 13, 40 ff., 166 ff., 194 f.
Analysis, 178 ff.
Argument, 49
Aristotelean logic, 10, 25, 47, 216 f.
Arithmetization, chap. III, § 4
Art, 148 ff., 156 ff., 184
Axiom of Reducibility, 65 ff.

Bernays, 21
Bernstein, B. A., 221 n.
Black, M., 169 n.
Boole, 10
Broad, C. D., 201 ff., 213
Brouwer, 16 n., 168

Calculus of predicates, 35. *See* Calculus of pure logic
Calculus of pure logic, chap. III, § 3
Calculus of unanalysed propositions, 34, chap. III, § 2
Carnap, R., 15, 20 n., 29 f., 38 f., 117 ff.
Category, 130, chap. IV, § 3, 147 f., 150, 180 f.
Church, A., 13 n., 21 n., 49 n., 72 f., 81 n.
Claim to truth. *See* Objective for reference
Class, 36 n., 133 n.
Communication, 126, 209, 215 f.
Completeness. *See* Decision-Problem

Comprehensiveness, 11
Concept, chap. IV, § 3
Conceptualization, 172 ff.
Contextual theory, 141 ff., 183 f., 190 ff.
Continuity, chap. V, § 2
Continuum, 159. *See* Continuity
Convention, chap. V, § 4
Curry, H., 13 n., 72, 75 f., 222

De Morgan, 10
Decision-Problem, chap. III
Dedekind, 63
Definite description. *See* Description
Denotation, 193
Description, 115, 118 n., 123, 131 f., 136, 160, 172 f., 176 ff., 181, 199
Dialectic, 147–51, 217
Discourse, 117, 119, 122–6, 156, 158 f., 170
Discreteness, 154 ff., 161
Disposition, 138, 160, 164, 172

Empirical proposition, 184 f., 192 f.
Epistemic attitude, 207
Equality, 35, 106
Equivalence, 35
Evaluation, 50 f.
Existential proposition, 50, chap. IV, § 2, 179
Expression, 175

Fact, 171 f., 201
Feys, R., 40 n.
Fitch, F., 42 n., 43 n.

Form, chap. I, § 3, 152, chap. V, § 3.
Formalism, 16 n., chap. II, § 6, chap. III
Functional theory, 182

Game, 152, 186 f., 195
Generality, 132
Generalization, 50 ff.
Geometry, 13, 166 ff.
Godel, K., 15, 77, chap. III, § 4, 187
Grelling, K., 61

Hegel, 146 ff.
Henle, P., 92 n.
Hilbert, 16 n., 23, 94 f.
Huntington, E., 42

Indeterminacy. *See* Continuity
Intensional logic. *See* Modality
Interpretation, 12, 91 f., 167 f., 205
Intuition, 26, 31 f. *See* Intuitional theory
Intuitional theory, 16 f., 25 f., 29, 34, 78, 86 f., 115, 155, 166, 170, 199
Intuitionism, 16 n., 166, 168

Johnson, W. E., 14 n., 207–9
Judgment, 207, 217 f. *See* Perceptual judgment

Kant, 9, 144 ff.

Langford, C. H., 58 n., 80 n., 186 n.
Language, 16 f., 121 ff.
Lewis, C. I., 42
Lindsay, R. B., 11 n.
Logical constant, 17

Logical paradox, chap. II
Logical positivism, 16 n., 173 n.
Logistic, 25
Lukasiewicz, 40, 61

Mark. *See* Symbol
Mathematics, 90
Matrix, 56
Meaning, 143 n., 205
Metalogic, 14 f., chap. I, § 2, 195–8
Modality, chap. I, § 4
Moody, E. A., 218 n.
Moore, G. E., 177
Multiplicity, 175 ff.

Name, 137–40, 177 ff.
Necessity, 135, 149 f., 157 f.
Normal form, 96
Number, 133 n., 179

Objective for reference, 123 ff., 130, 133, 208 f.
Occam, William, 24 f., 218 n.
Operationalism. *See* Pragmatism
Order, 55, 175 f.
Otherness, 153 ff.

Paradox of objective reference, 117
Peano, 10
Peirce, C. S., 10
Perception, 162 ff., 165, 172 f., 221
Perceptual judgment, 123 ff., 133 n., chap. VI, § 3
Postulational system, 11 f.
Postulational theory, 16 ff., 154 f., 197. *See* Formalism
Potentiality. *See* Disposition
Pragmatism, 173 n., 182 ff.
Predicate, 49

Index

Predication, 217
Presentation, 123 ff.
Primitive proposition, 25, 87
Principle of Extensionality, chap. I, § 4
Principle of the excluded middle, 152, 166, 168, 188 f., 194
Principle of non-contradition, chap. V, § 1, 163, 166, 188 f., 191, 194, 201 f.
Proposition, 171, 175, chap. VI
Propositional function, 36 n., 49, 196 n.

Quine, W. V., 71 f., 74 f., 190 ff., 193 n.

Ramsey, F., 53 n., 62, 67, chap. II, § 5, 77 f., 81
Real number, 63 ff.
Recursive function, 109, 111 n.
Reichenbach, 142 n.
Robinson, R., 204 n.
Ross, W. D., 218 *n*.
Rule, 139 f., 160, 184–8, 195 f., 212, 214 f.
Russell, B., 10, 30, 47 ff., 50 n., chap. II, §§ 2 & 3, 65, 69, 71, 78 ff., 84 f., 118 n., 126 n., 128 f., 133 n., 141, 176, 178–81
Ryle, 204 n.

Schema, 20 f., 92 n., 145
Schönfinkel, 222

Schröder, 10
Science, 11 f.
Semantics, 23, 120 ff.
Sentence, 171, 202, 221 f.
Significance, 26 ff., 47 ff., 152 f.
Statement, 216
Symbols, 14, 17, 29, 155, 194, 198
Syntax-language, 27 ff., 171. *See* Metalogic

Tarski, A., 15, 23, 120 ff.
Term, 216 f.
Theory of logic, 14. *See* Metalogic
Theory of types, chap. II, § 2, 131
Thought, 148, chap. VI, § 4
Transcendental logic, chap. IV, § 4
Truth, 174, 190 ff., 206
Truth-function, 198 f.
Truth-table, 95, 194
Truth-value, 35, 206, 211, 215 f., 220 n.
Type. *See* Theory of types

Undecidable proposition, 113
Universal, 181

Vagueness, 169 n.
Value, 151, 158
Variable, 17
"Vicious-circle" principle, 33, 113

Waismann, F., 210–14
Whitehead, A., 69, 206 ff.
Wittgenstein, 19 *n.*, 33, 170 *n.*

For Product Safety Concerns and Information please contact our EU
representative GPSR@taylorandfrancis.com
Taylor & Francis Verlag GmbH, Kaufingerstraße 24, 80331 München, Germany

www.ingramcontent.com/pod-product-compliance
Lightning Source LLC
Chambersburg PA
CBHW052109300426
44116CB00010B/1597